Building RESTful Web Services with Java EE 8

Create modern RESTful web services with the Java EE 8 API

Mario-Leander Reimer

BIRMINGHAM - MUMBAI

Building RESTful Web Services with Java EE 8

Commissioning Editor: Richa Tripathi
Acquisition Editor: Denim Pinto
Content Development Editor: Priyanka Sawant
Technical Editor: Romy Dias
Copy Editor: Safis Editing
Project Coordinator: Vaidehi Sawant
Proofreader: Safis Editing
Indexer: Mariammal Chettiyar
Graphics: Jason Monteiro
Production Coordinator: Shantanu Zagade

First published: July 2018

Production reference: 1300718

Published by Packt Publishing Ltd.
Livery Place
35 Livery Street
Birmingham
B3 2PB, UK.

ISBN 978-1-78953-288-3

www.packtpub.com

`mapt.io`

Mapt is an online digital library that gives you full access to over 5,000 books and videos, as well as industry leading tools to help you plan your personal development and advance your career. For more information, please visit our website.

Why subscribe?

- Spend less time learning and more time coding with practical eBooks and Videos from over 4,000 industry professionals

- Improve your learning with Skill Plans built especially for you

- Get a free eBook or video every month

- Mapt is fully searchable

- Copy and paste, print, and bookmark content

PacktPub.com

Did you know that Packt offers eBook versions of every book published, with PDF and ePub files available? You can upgrade to the eBook version at `www.PacktPub.com` and as a print book customer, you are entitled to a discount on the eBook copy. Get in touch with us at `service@packtpub.com` for more details.

At `www.PacktPub.com`, you can also read a collection of free technical articles, sign up for a range of free newsletters, and receive exclusive discounts and offers on Packt books and eBooks.

Contributors

About the author

Mario-Leander Reimer is a chief technologist for QAware GmbH. He is a senior Java developer with several years' experience in designing complex and large-scale system architectures. He continuously looks for innovations and ways to combine and apply state-of-the-art technology and open source software components to real-world customer projects. He studied computer science at Rosenheim and Staffordshire University and he teaches cloud computing as a part-time lecturer.

About the reviewer

Luca Stancapiano has been working in the IT industry since 2000. He specializes in Java EE and JBoss, and has collaborated with Apache, Alfresco, Atlassian, and eXo on several open source products. He lives in Italy and collaborates with leading consulting companies on the design and implementation of applications for both government and private companies. He brings projects such as WildFly, Alfresco ECM, Activiti, JGroups, Arquillian, eXo Portal, Solr, Infinispan, JBoss Portal, GateIn, Jira, and Confluence, and manages Vige, an open source community specializing in open government and smart cities. He is one of the authors of *GateIn Cookbook*, by Packt Publishing.

Packt is searching for authors like you

If you're interested in becoming an author for Packt, please visit `authors.packtpub.com` and apply today. We have worked with thousands of developers and tech professionals, just like you, to help them share their insight with the global tech community. You can make a general application, apply for a specific hot topic that we are recruiting an author for, or submit your own idea.

Table of Contents

Preface

Java Enterprise Edition is one of the leading application programming platforms for enterprise Java development. With Java EE 8 finally released and the first application servers being available, it is time to have a closer look at how to develop modern and lightweight web services with the latest API additions and improvements.

This book is a comprehensive guide that shows you how to develop state-of-the-art RESTful web services with the latest Java EE 8 APIs. We start by giving an overview of Java EE 8 and the latest API additions and improvements. Then, you will implement, build, and package your first working web service as a prototype for the remainder of the book. It delves into the details of implementing synchronous RESTful web services and clients with JAX-RS. Next up, you will learn about the specifics of data binding and content marshaling using the JSON-B 1.0 and JSON-P 1.1 APIs. You will then learn how to leverage the power of asynchronous APIs on both the server and client sides, and you will learn how to use **Server-Sent Events (SSEs)** for PUSH communications. The final chapter covers some advanced web service topics, such as validation, JWT security, and diagnosing web services.

By the end of this book, you will have a thorough understanding of the Java EE 8 APIs required for lightweight web service development. Also, you will have implemented several working web services to provide you with the required practical experience.

Who this book is for

This book is intended for Java developers who want to learn how to implement web services using the latest Java EE 8 APIs. No prior knowledge of Java EE 8 is required; experience with a previous Java EE version will, however, be beneficial.

What this book covers

Chapter 1, *Getting Started with Java EE 8*, gets you started with Java EE 8—we'll implement our first simple web service using Java EE 8 and the relevant APIs.

Chapter 2, *Building Synchronous Web Services and Clients*, dives deep into synchronous services—we'll be implementing synchronous web services, and also web service clients, using the relevant APIs.

Chapter 3, *Content Marshaling with JSON-B and JSON-P*, covers content marshaling—we'll be using JSON-B and JSON-P for marshaling our content.

Chapter 4, *Building Asynchronous Web Services*, explores asynchronous services—we'll be implementing asynchronous web services, and also a web service client, using the new reactive client APIs.

Chapter 5, *Using Server-Sent Events (SSE)*, covers SSEs—we'll be implementing PUSH notifications using those services and events.

Chapter 6, *Advanced REST APIs*, gives you an overview of some more advanced REST APIs—we'll be implementing Design by Contract, we'll talk about JSON Web Token security, and we'll also add the ability to diagnose our web services.

To get the most out of this book

You need the following to get the most out of this book:

- You need to have basic programming skills and some Java knowledge is required
- You need a computer with a modern operating system, such as Windows 10, macOS, or Linux
- You need a working Java 8 language installation; we'll be using Maven 3.5.x as our build tool
- We'll be using Payara Server 5.x as our Java 8 application server
- You need Docker for Windows, macOS, or Linux
- You need an IDE with Java EE 8 support, such as IntelliJ IDEA 2017.3, and you will need a REST client, such as Postman or SoapUI

Download the example code files

You can download the example code files for this book from your account at www.packtpub.com. If you purchased this book elsewhere, you can visit www.packtpub.com/support and register to have the files emailed directly to you.

You can download the code files by following these steps:

1. Log in or register at www.packtpub.com.
2. Select the **SUPPORT** tab.
3. Click on **Code Downloads & Errata**.
4. Enter the name of the book in the **Search** box and follow the onscreen instructions.

Once the file is downloaded, please make sure that you unzip or extract the folder using the latest version of:

- WinRAR/7-Zip for Windows
- Zipeg/iZip/UnRarX for Mac
- 7-Zip/PeaZip for Linux

The code bundle for the book is also hosted on GitHub at https://github.com/PacktPublishing/Building-RESTful-Web-Services-with-Java-EE-8. In case there's an update to the code, it will be updated on the existing GitHub repository.

We also have other code bundles from our rich catalog of books and videos available at https://github.com/PacktPublishing/. Check them out!

Conventions used

There are a number of text conventions used throughout this book.

CodeInText: Indicates code words in text, database table names, folder names, filenames, file extensions, pathnames, dummy URLs, user input, and Twitter handles. Here is an example: "In the preceding Dockerfile, we mentioned that we're using payara/server-full."

A block of code is set as follows:

```
<dependency>
    <groupId>javax</groupId>
    <artifactId>javaee-api</artifactId>
    <version>8.0</version>
    <scope>provided</scope>
</dependency>
```

When we wish to draw your attention to a particular part of a code block, the relevant lines or items are set in bold:

```
@PUT
@Path("/{isbn}")
public Response update(@PathParam("isbn") String isbn, Book book) {
    if (!Objects.equals(isbn, book.getIsbn())) {
```

Any command-line input or output is written as follows:

```
>docker build -t hello-javaee8:1.0 .
```

Bold: Indicates a new term, an important word, or words that you see onscreen. For example, words in menus or dialog boxes appear in the text like this. Here is an example: "Let's check our browser, you should see the **"Hello World."** message."

 Warnings or important notes appear like this.

 Tips and tricks appear like this.

Get in touch

Feedback from our readers is always welcome.

General feedback: Email `feedback@packtpub.com` and mention the book title in the subject of your message. If you have questions about any aspect of this book, please email us at `questions@packtpub.com`.

Errata: Although we have taken every care to ensure the accuracy of our content, mistakes do happen. If you have found a mistake in this book, we would be grateful if you would report this to us. Please visit `www.packtpub.com/submit-errata`, selecting your book, clicking on the Errata Submission Form link, and entering the details.

Piracy: If you come across any illegal copies of our works in any form on the Internet, we would be grateful if you would provide us with the location address or website name. Please contact us at `copyright@packtpub.com` with a link to the material.

If you are interested in becoming an author: If there is a topic that you have expertise in and you are interested in either writing or contributing to a book, please visit `authors.packtpub.com`.

Reviews

Please leave a review. Once you have read and used this book, why not leave a review on the site that you purchased it from? Potential readers can then see and use your unbiased opinion to make purchase decisions, we at Packt can understand what you think about our products, and our authors can see your feedback on their book. Thank you!

For more information about Packt, please visit `packtpub.com`.

Getting Started with Java EE 8 1

In this first chapter, you will learn why Java EE is a great platform for building lightweight state-of-the-art microservices. You will learn the latest advances in the different APIs of Java EE 8, with a focus on the more microservice-relevant APIs. You will then learn how to develop, build, run, and package your first microservice powered by Java EE 8.

This chapter includes the following sections:

- Why is Java EE a good platform for microservices?
- What's new in Java EE 8?
- Getting started with Java EE 8 microservices
- Containerizing Java EE 8 microservices using Docker

Technical requirements

You need basic programming skills and some Java knowledge. Along with that, you need a computer with a modern operating system, such as Windows 10, macOS, or Linux. We'll be using Maven 3.5 as our build tool and Payara Server as our application server. For the Java 8 application server, you need Docker for Windows, Mac or Linux, an IDE with Java EE 8 support, such as IntelliJ, and a REST client, such as Postman or SoapUI.

Why is Java EE a good platform for microservices?

Well, this is the question, why? And the short answer is simple: because Java EE 8 is the most lightweight enterprise framework currently out there. Let me give you a few more details. First up, Java EE is an industry standard. It's been developed by a vendor-neutral committee and there is widespread knowledge out there because Java EE has been available for a couple of years already. Java EE consists of several specifications, and these specifications have very tight integration. Also, Java EE applies a convention of a configuration programming model, which means that you don't need cumbersome XML descriptors anymore; just throw in a couple of annotations and you're done. For most of the services you're going to develop, you will not need any external dependencies, and this leads to thin deployment artifacts. And finally, you have the availability of modern application servers that suit the cloud era.

Java EE version history

If you have a look at the Java EE version history, which you can find at `https://en.wikipedia.org/wiki/Java_Platform,_Enterprise_Edition`, you'll see we've come a long way since J2EE 1.2 was first released on December 12, 1999. If you look on the far-right side in the following diagram, you can see Java EE 8 was released on September 21, 2017, which means we have 18 years of experience and 18 years of community-built knowledge. Therefore it's definitely a very mature and stable API that's been continually improved:

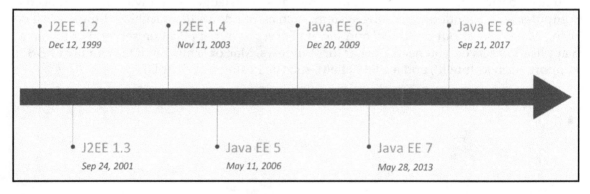

Java EE version history

Overview of Java EE 8

In the following diagram, you can see an overview of Java EE 8 in its current state, you have loads of APIs here that you can program against, and it should meet most of the needs of any enterprise's web-service development. You've got JPA for persistence, JMS for messaging, good JAX-WS for web services in structure, JAX-RS for REST services, and many more APIs you can use for your modern enterprise's application development:

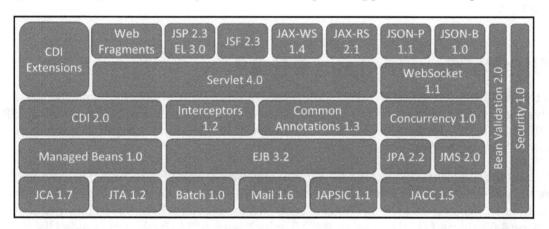

Overview of Java EE 8

And all you need is the following code, which is the only dependency required; this is the Maven dependency for the Java EE 8 API and leads to no external dependencies. All you need is Java EE 8 and Java 8; this results in very thin artifacts which speeds up your daily development and your deployment cycles, and because you have those thin WAR files, this is very Docker-friendly:

```
<dependency>
    <groupId>javax</groupId>
    <artifactId>javaee-api</artifactId>
    <version>8.0</version>
    <scope>provided</scope>
</dependency>
```

Now there are people out there who say that Java EE 8, especially the application service, should not go in a Docker container, but those heavy times are over; modern application servers are really lightweight, have a look at Payara server or WildFly Swarm, or maybe Open Liberty or Apache TomEE, along with the various other application servers. These servers are very lightweight and are definitely suitable to be run in a Docker container. I hope by now you're convinced that Java EE 8 is indeed the most lightweight enterprise framework currently available. In the next section, we're going to have a look what's new in Java EE 8.

What's new in Java EE 8?

In this section, we're going to take a look at the different APIs of Java EE 8 and the latest advances, with a focus on the more microservice-relevant APIs. We're going to look at JSR 370, which is JAX-RS 2.1; JSR 367, which is the JSON Binding; and also JSR 374, which is the Java API for JSON Processing.

We saw the different APIs in Java EE 8 in the *Overview of Java EE 8* section. The ones in blue are the ones that have been added or revamped. We see that CDI is been bumped to version 2.0, mainly focusing on asynchronous events, and the Servlet API has been bumped to version 4.0, adding HTTP2 support. JSF 2.3, which is an API to build server-side UIs, the old JSF bean-managed model, has been removed and it's fully integrated with CDI. On the right-hand side of the figure in the previous section, you see the Bean Validation API, which has been bumped to version 2.0. It's tightly integrated with CDI and has been revamped to fully support Java 8 features such as streams and lambdas. There's also a totally new Security API for cloud security and past security in adding standardized authorization, authentication mechanisms, and APIs. Here, we want to focus on JAX-RS 2.1, JSON-P 1.1, and JSON-B 1.0.

Let's get started with JAX-RS 2.1. First, it improved the integration with CDI, so all your resource beans are properly CDI-managed. It's also been tightly integrated with JSON-B for JSON marshalling and JSON-P for JSON Processing. Also, server-sent events have been added to implement push notifications. They support non-blocking I/O and all the providers, such as filters and interceptors for JAX-RS. There's also been an improved JAX-RS, which is a synchronous client API supporting a completion stage. If you have a look at the Java API for JSON Processing, it's been updated to version 1.1 to support JSON Pointer and JSON Patch. It allows you to edit and transform operations for your JSON object model, and the API has been updated to work with Java SE 8 features, such as lambdas and streams.

The new kid on the block is JSON-B, the JSON Binding 1.0 API. It's the new standard way to convert JSON into Java objects and vice-versa. For a long time, we've had JSON-B to do the same for XML, and JSON-B is the API to do that for JSON. JSON-B leverages JSON-P and provides a conversion layer above it. It provides a default mapping algorithm for converting existing Java classes to JSON. The mapping is highly customizable through the use of Java annotations, and you can plug in different JSON-B runtimes to convert Java objects to and from JSON, such as Jackson. Those are the most relevant Java EE 8 APIs with respect to web-service development. In the next section, we're getting started with Java EE 8 microservices development.

Getting started with Java EE 8 microservices

In this section, we're going to take a look at the following things:

- How to develop, build, and run your first Java-EE-8-powered microservice
- Required Java EE 8 dependencies for basic web-service development
- Basic components of any JAX-RS-based web service
- Deployment of a thin WAR artifact using Payara Server 5

Let's get started and dive into the code. I've prepared my IDE and a raw skeleton Maven project. What you see here is a very basic POM file:

There's one thing missing though; first, we need to define the required dependency for the Java EE 8 API. Let's do that:

```xml
<dependency>
    <groupId>javax</groupId>
    <artifactId>javaee-api</artifactId>
    <version>8.0</version>
    <scope>provided</scope>
</dependency>
```

We specify `version` as `8.0`. We should also define the proper `scope` for this, which is `provided` in this case because the Java EE 8 API will later be provided by our application server and we are done with our dependency. Next, we should add a `beans.xml` descriptor to the `WEB-INF` directory of our web application:

```xml
<?xml version="1.0" encoding="UTF-8"?>
<beans xmlns="http://xmlns.jcp.org/xml/ns/javaee"
       xmlns:xsi="http://www.w3.org/2001/XMLSchema-instance"
       xsi:schemaLocation="http://xmlns.jcp.org/xml/ns/javaee
                    http://xmlns.jcp.org/xml/ns/javaee/beans_1_1.xsd"
       bean-discovery-mode="all">
</beans>
```

We do this and we're done, what's next? Well, next we should bootstrap our JAX-RS application. Now let's create a class called `JAXRSConfiguration`. The name really doesn't matter. What's important is that this class extends from the `Application` base class. Bear in mind the `javax.ws.rs.core` package while selecting the `Application`. It's also important that you specify the `@ApplicationPath` annotation. This will be the base path our REST API will be accessible under, thus we call that `"api"`:

```java
package com.packtpub.javaee8;

import javax.ws.rs.ApplicationPath;
import javax.ws.rs.core.Application;

/**
 * Configures a JAX-RS endpoint.
 */
@ApplicationPath("api")
public class JAXRSConfiguration extends Application {
}
```

Once we've bootstrapped JAX-RS, what's missing is a proper REST resource. Let's create a class called `HelloWorldResouce`. We used the `@Path` annotation, which will be the path this resource will be accessible under. We'll call that `"hello"`. Next up, we create a method that will produce the proper response once called, we call that `helloWorld`. We use the proper `Response` here. We annotate this using the `@GET` annotation because we will be issuing `GET` requests later on, and we'll say that it produces `MediaType.APPLICATION_JSON`. Then we return `Response.ok`, where `ok` is HTTP status 200 of a response when we call the `build`. So, what should be used as the response? We'll be using `Map<String, String>` as our response and will return `singletonMap` with the `message` key and the `Hello World` value:

```
package com.packtpub.javaee8;

import javax.ws.rs.GET;
import javax.ws.rs.Path;
import javax.ws.rs.Produces;
import javax.ws.rs.core.MediaType;
import javax.ws.rs.core.Response;
import java.util.Map;

import static java.util.Collections.singletonMap;

/**
 * The REST resource implementation class.
 */
@Path("hello")
public class HelloWorldResource {
    @GET
    @Produces(MediaType.APPLICATION_JSON)
    public Response helloWorld() {
        Map<String, String> response = singletonMap("message",
          "Building Web Services with Java EE 8.");
        return Response.ok(response) .build();
    }
}
```

We should already have a very simple working microservice. Now let's deploy this onto our Payara Server 5 and run it. We're going to deploy the WAR file, it's been built; you can see that it's already been deployed and the deployment took 5.1 milliseconds.

Let's check our browser. You should see the **"Hello World."** message, as shown in the following screenshot:

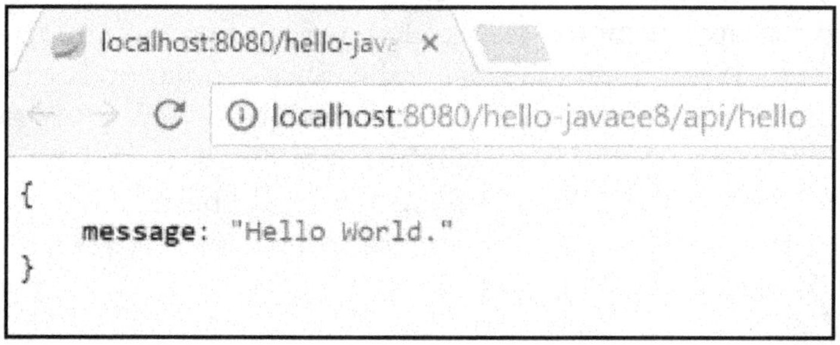

If you don't trust me, let's just modify the value here to `"Building Web Services with Java EE 8."` value. We deploy this once more and update our artifact. The new version has been deployed. Let's go back to our browser to check that we have the proper response message, as shown in the following screenshot:

That's all for this section; in the next section, I'm going to show you how to containerize your Java EE 8 microservice.

Containerizing Java EE 8 microservices

In this section, we're going to take a look at how to containerize and run our Java EE 8 microservice using Docker. We'll learn how to write a basic Docker file, and we'll also see how to build and run the Docker image using Payara Server full and Payara Server micro edition. Let's open our IDE again to the microservice project from the previous section; all that's missing here is `Dockerfile`, therefore let's create one.

Now the question is: what base image should we use? We have two basic options when using Payara: you can either use the server-full image or the Payara micro edition. Let's use the full version of Payara first. `Dockerfile` will be as follows:

```
FROM payara/server-full:5-SNAPSHOT

COPY target/hello-javaee8.war $DEPLOY_DIR
```

In the preceding `Dockerfile`, we mentioned that we're using `payara/server-full`. We need to use the correct version of it, in our case this is version `5-SNAPSHOT`, and then copy the `hello-javaee8.war` file of our microservice into the correct location of the produced image. We need to issue a `COPY` command from `target/hello-javaee8.war` and then copy this into the deployment directory, that should be it, let's see whether is worked. We open a console, making sure that we're in the right directory. We check that everything is packaged nicely, and to do this we call `mvn package` just to make sure the WAR file is in the correct state. If it is, you'll see my things running while compiling, an absence of tests, and the WAR file is up to date:

```
--- maven-resources-plugin:2.6:testResources (default-testResources) @ hello-javaee8 -
Using 'UTF-8' encoding to copy filtered resources.
skip non existing resourceDirectory J:\codebase\hello-javaee8\src\test\resources

--- maven-compiler-plugin:3.1:testCompile (default-testCompile) @ hello-javaee8 ---
No sources to compile

--- maven-surefire-plugin:2.12.4:test (default-test) @ hello-javaee8 ---
No tests to run.

--- maven-war-plugin:2.2:war (default-war) @ hello-javaee8 ---
Packaging webapp
Assembling webapp [hello-javaee8] in [J:\codebase\hello-javaee8\target\hello-javaee8]
Processing war project
Copying webapp resources [J:\codebase\hello-javaee8\src\main\webapp]
Webapp assembled in [128 msecs]
Building war: J:\codebase\hello-javaee8\target\hello-javaee8.war
------------------------------------------------------------------------
BUILD SUCCESS
------------------------------------------------------------------------
Total time: 11.030 s
Finished at: 2018-01-11T10:04:47+01:00
```

We build Docker using `-t`, which specifies the tag we want to use, we do that by calling `hello-javaee8` and we give it a version number, `1.0`:

```
>docker build -t hello-javaee8:1.0 .
```

Using the following command, let's see whether our server starts up:

```
>docker run -it -p 8080:8080 hello-javaee8:1.0
```

We mapped port 8080 from the container onto our Docker host. You'll see that the Payara GlassFish Server is starting up in the console—it should only take a couple of seconds—and in a second we should see that our application is deployed. To check that we can reach our web service hit the IP address as shown in the following screenshot. This is the IP address of my Docker host port 8080 and we can access our service, which was successful:

Now let's stop that and delete the contents of this Dockerfile. I want to show you how to use the Payara micro edition instead. First, we need to change FROM. To do this we use a different base tag for this image (payara/micro:5-SNAPSHOT), and then copy the hello-javaee8.war file into the proper location for this base image. Next we copy our WAR file in the target directory and we call it to our /opt/payara/deployments. This is the default deployments directory for the micro edition base container. The Dockerfile should look as follows:

```
FROM payara/micro:5-SNAPSHOT

COPY target/hello-javaee8.war /opt/payara/deployments
```

Switch back to the console and issue the Docker build command again:

```
>docker build -t hello-javaee8:1.0 .
```

Fire up the container again:

```
>docker run -it -p 8080:8080 hello-javaee8:1.0
```

You can see that the output in the console changes and we're using the Payara micro runtime this time. This takes a couple of seconds to spin up our web service, and in a few seconds it should be done. We can see that our REST Endpoints are available. Let's check again. We go to our management console and we can see that we have a running container. Try calling the web service from the browser, as shown in the following screenshot:

We can see that everything's working fine and we have a running Dockerized version of our web service.

Summary

In this chapter, we talked about Java EE and the fact that it's a great platform for building modern and lightweight web services. We had a look at the different APIs of Java EE 8 and the latest advances, with a focus on the more microservice-relevant APIs, such as JAX-RS, JSON-B, and JSON-P. We then developed, built, and ran our Java-EE-8-powered microservice and deployed it locally to the Payara Server. In the final section, we containerized and ran our Java EE 8 microservice using Docker.

In the next chapter, we'll do a deep dive into building synchronous web services and clients using the relevant JAX-RS APIs.

2
Building Synchronous Web Services and Clients

In this chapter, we will go into the details of building synchronous microservices with Java EE 8. We will learn how to implement server-side REST APIs using basic JAX-RS annotations, implement sub-resource locators for nested REST APIs, and use HTTP status codes and exception mappers for exception handling. You will also learn how to implement the client side using JAX-RS client APIs, and finally, we will have a look at different test strategies for Java EE web services.

We'll cover the following sections in this chapter:

- Implementing basic REST APIs with JAX-RS
- Using sub-resources
- Error handling in JAX-RS
- Implementing web service clients with Java EE 8
- Testing Java EE 8 web services

By the end of this chapter, we'll have implemented a small library microservice that offers a REST API for books, authors, and loans. We'll implement the library client as a standalone application and use the Jersey Test Framework and the Test Containers framework to test our REST API.

Implementing basic REST APIs with JAX-RS

In this section, we're going to take a look at how to implement a REST resource using basic JAX-RS annotations. I'll show you how you can inject and use CDI beans in your JAX-RS resource implementation and show you how to properly use HTTP methods to model CRUD semantics, and of course we'll be running the web service within a Docker container:

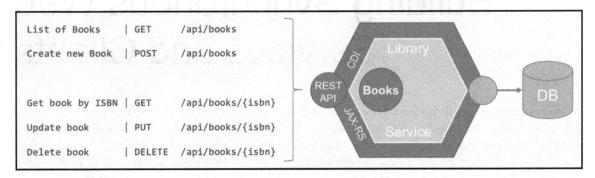

Conceptual view of this section

We'll implement a REST API to get a list of books so that we'll be able to create new books, get a book by ISBN, update books, and delete a book.

We will create a basic project skeleton and prepare a simple class, which is called `BookResource`, and we will use this to implement the CRUD REST API for our books. So first up, we need to annotate our class using the proper annotations. We will use the `@Path` annotation to specify the path for our books API, which is `"books"`, and we make a `@RequestScoped` CDI bean. Now, to implement our business logic, we want to use another CDI bean, thus we need to get it injected into this one. This other CDI bean is called `bookshelf`, and we'll use the usual CDI `@Inject` annotation to get a reference to our `bookshelf`. Next up, we want to implement a method to get hold of a list of all books, so let's do that. What you see here is we have a `books` method, which is `@GET` annotated, and it produces `MediaType.APPLICATION_JSON` and returns a JAX-RS response. You can see that we construct a response of `ok`, which is HTTP 200; as the body, we use `bookshelf.findAll`, which is a collection of books, and then we build the response. The `BookResource.java` file should look as follows:

```
@Path("books")
@RequestScoped
public class BookResource {

    @Inject
    private Bookshelf bookshelf;
```

```
@GET
@Produces(MediaType.APPLICATION_JSON)
public Response books() {
    return Response.ok(bookshelf.findAll()).build();
}
```

Next up, we want to implement a GET message to get a specific book. To do that, again we have a @GET annotated method, but this time we have the @Path annotation with the "/{isbn}" parameter. To get hold of this parameter, which is called the isbn, we use the @PathParam annotation to pass the value. We use bookshelf to find our book by ISBN and return the book found using the HTTP status code 200, that is, ok:

```
@GET
@Path("/{isbn}")
public Response get(@PathParam("isbn") String isbn) {
    Book book = bookshelf.findByISBN(isbn);
    return Response.ok(book).build();
}
```

Next up, we want to create books. In order to create something, it's a convention to use HTTP POST as a method. We consume the application JSON and we expect the JSON structure of a book, we call bookshelf.create with the book parameter, and then we use UriBuilder to construct the URI for the just-created book; this is also a convention. We then return this URI using Response.created, which matches the HTTP status code 201, and we'll call build() to build the final response:

```
@POST
@Consumes(MediaType.APPLICATION_JSON)
public Response create(Book book) {
    if (bookshelf.exists(book.getIsbn())) {
        return Response.status(Response.Status.CONFLICT).build();
    }

    bookshelf.create(book);
    URI location = UriBuilder.fromResource(BookResource.class)
            .path("/{isbn}")
            .resolveTemplate("isbn", book.getIsbn())
            .build();
    return Response.created(location).build();
}
```

Next up, we'll implement the update method for an existing book. To update things, again it's a convention to use the HTTP method PUT. We update this by putting in a specific location. Again, we use the @Path parameter with a value of "/{isbn}". We give a reference to this isbn here in the update method parameter, and we have the JSON structure of our book ready. We use bookshelf.update to update the book and in the end we return the status code ok:

```
@PUT
@Path("/{isbn}")
public Response update(@PathParam("isbn") String isbn, Book book) {
    bookshelf.update(isbn, book);
    return Response.ok().build();
}
```

Finally, we're going to implement the delete message, and as you might expect, we use the HTTP method DELETE on the path of an identified ISBN. Again, we use the @PathParam annotation here, we call bookshelf.delete, and we return ok if everything went well:

```
@DELETE
@Path("/{isbn}")
public Response delete(@PathParam("isbn") String isbn) {
    bookshelf.delete(isbn);
    return Response.ok().build();
}
```

This is our CRUD implementation for our book resource. I told you that we're going to use a Docker container and the Payara Server micro edition to run everything. We will copy our WAR file to the deployments directory and then we're up and running:

```
FROM payara/micro:5-SNAPSHOT

COPY target/library-service.war /opt/payara/deployments
```

Let's see if everything's running on our REST client (Postman).

First up, we get a list of books. As you can see here, this works as expected:

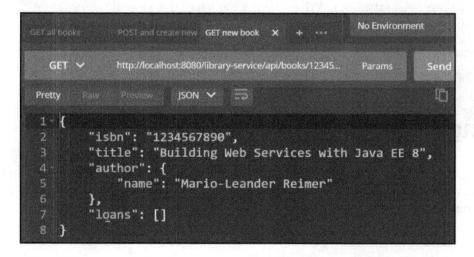

```
39      ]
40    },
41    {
42        "isbn": "1786469200",
43        "title": "Mastering Java EE 8 Application Development",
44        "author": {
45            "name": "Kapila Bogahapitiya,  Sandeep Nair"
46        },
47        "loans": [
48            {
49                "id": "44adb4ec-3263-4477-b182-d3107019d3d9",
50                "username": "mario-leander.reimer@qaware.de"
51            }
52        ]
53    }
```

If we want to create a new book, we issue the **POST and create new book** request, and you'll see a status code of **OK 200**. We get the new book by using **GET new book**; this is the book we just created, as shown in the following screenshot:

```
1 {
2    "isbn": "1234567890",
3    "title": "Building Web Services with Java EE 8",
4    "author": {
5        "name": "Mario-Leander Reimer"
6    },
7    "loans": []
8 }
```

We can update the book by using **Update new book**, and we'll get a status code of **OK 200**. We can get the updated book again by using **GET new book**; we get the updated title, as shown in the following screenshot:

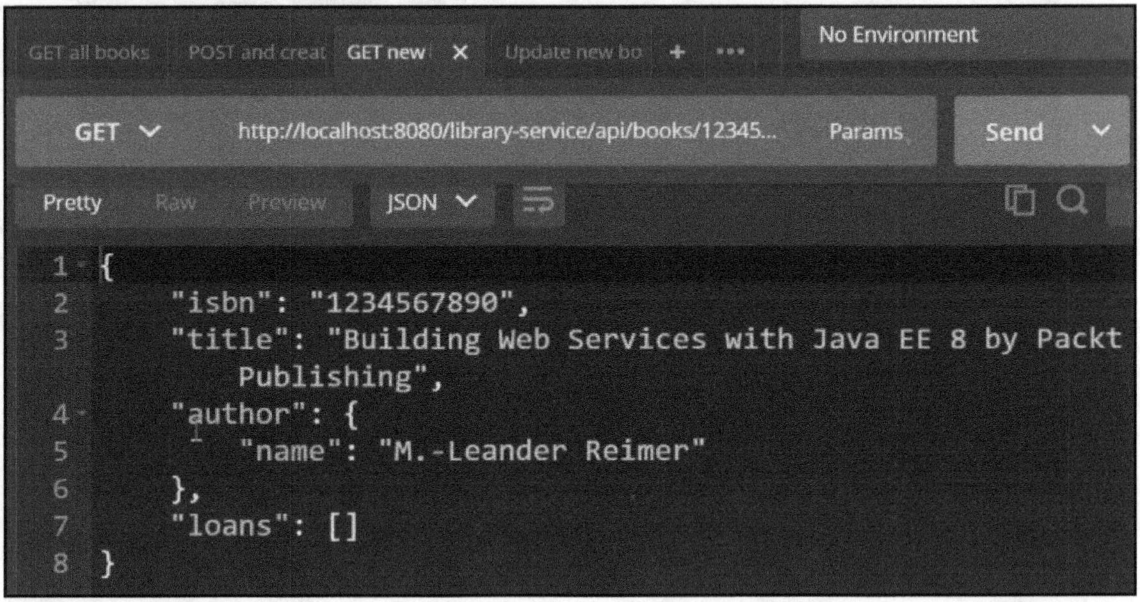

Finally, we can delete the book. When we get the list of books again, our newly created book is not part of the list of books anymore.

In the next section, we're going to have a look at how we can use sub-resources and sub-resource locators.

Using sub-resources

In this section, we're going to take a look at how to implement simple sub-resource locator methods. We'll have a look at how you can obtain CDI sub-resource instances from the root resource, and we're going to have a look at how you can pass context information from the root to the sub-resources:

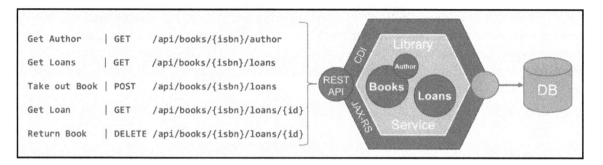

```
Get Author    | GET    /api/books/{isbn}/author
Get Loans     | GET    /api/books/{isbn}/loans
Take out Book | POST   /api/books/{isbn}/loans
Get Loan      | GET    /api/books/{isbn}/loans/{id}
Return Book   | DELETE /api/books/{isbn}/loans/{id}
```

Conceptual view of this section

Books have authors, and they can be lent out. In this section, what we'll do is provide specific REST endpoints to obtain the author of a book and the loan details of the books. We have prepared the skeleton of the project, as shown in the following screenshot:

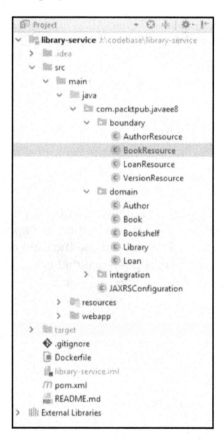

Let's start with the authors. In `BookResource.java`, add a resource locator method. A resource locator method is a simple method that is only annotated using the `@Path` annotation. In this case, we use `@Path("/{isbn}/author")`. The `return` type of a resource locator method is another resource. In this case, it's the `AuthorResource` locator method. Thus, we create the `AuthorResource` locator:

```
@Path("/{isbn}/author")
public AuthorResource author(@PathParam("isbn") String isbn) {
    Book book = bookshelf.findByISBN(isbn);
    return new AuthorResource(book);
}
```

It produces `APPLICATION_JSON`. We get a reference to our book in the constructor. Next up in this sub-resource, we can add the usual `GET`, `POST`, or `PUT` annotated HTTP methods again. In this case, we have one `GET` method annotated, which gets the author of our book:

```
@Produces(MediaType.APPLICATION_JSON)
public class AuthorResource {
    private final Book book;

    AuthorResource(Book book) {
        this.book = book;
    }

    @GET
    public Author get() {
        return book.getAuthor();
    }
}
```

This is really straightforward for simple resources, but what if we want to use CDI injection? If we want to do that, we need to take a different approach. First, we need to get a reference to `ResourceContext`; make sure you use the right one. By using this `ResourceContext`, we can get hold of a reference that is fully CDI injected. Again, we annotated using `@Path`, returned `loanResource`, and this time we used `context.getResource` from `LoanResource.class`. This returns a fully injected `loanResource` instance:

```
@RequestScoped
public class BookResource {

    @Inject
    private Bookshelf bookshelf;
    @Context
    private ResourceContext context;
    @Path("/{isbn}/loans")
```

```
public LoanResource loans(@PathParam("isbn") String isbn) {
    LoanResource loanResource =
    context.getResource(LoanResource.class);
    loanResource.setIsbn(isbn);

    return loanResource;
}
}
```

We then populate `LoanResource` using the `@Path("/{isbn}")` parameter. Now, the important bit: because we did this, you really need to make sure that this instance is `@RequestScoped`. This is because we pass in the `isbn` and here you can implement the usual REST resource methods we need for `LoanResource`.

In this case, for example, we will get the specific loan, and we can return a book, we can lend a book to create a loan.

If we switch to a REST client (Postman) and we want to obtain the book author by using the **GET book author** request, and click on **Send** and only the author is returned, as shown in the following screenshot:

We can obtain a list of loans, as shown in the following screenshot:

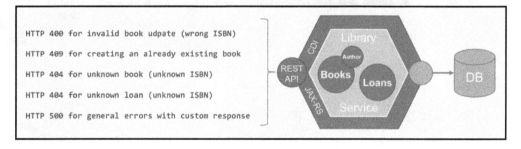

We can delete a loan, which means that the book has been returned, we can add new loans, and so on and so forth.

In the next section, we're going to cover how to perform error handling in JAX-RS.

Error handling in JAX-RS

In this section, we're going to take a look at handling user and server-side errors in a RESTful way by using an appropriate HTTP status code, for example, HTTP status code 400 Bad Request for invalid and malformed requests, status 404 Not Found if something could not be found, and HTTP status code 500 Internal Server Error if something happens unexpectedly. We'll also see how to use `WebApplicationException` and its subclasses to model error handling, and finally we'll be implementing a custom `ExceptionMappers` to handle runtime exceptions and return custom error responses:

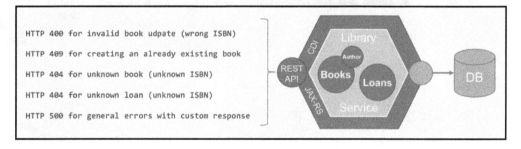

Conceptual view of this section

This is what we'll do conceptually in this section: we'll again extend our library microservice by several HTTP status codes , for example, HTTP 400 if you issue an invalid book update, 409 for creating an already existing book, 404 for unknown books and loans, and HTTP status code 500 for general errors with a custom response.

Let's switch to our IDE and return to `BookResource` again. Here, we haven't taken much care of proper error handling so far. As you can see in `bookshelf.create(book)`, for example, we create the book without checking whether the book already exists. The simplest way is to perform the checking before you do any work. To do that, we use our `bookshelf` to check whether the book—or to be more precise, the ISBN of the book—already exists, and if it does, we return a custom status code and we set the status to `CONFLICT`, which is 409, and the error response will be returned immediately. This is the most basic form of error handling, by returning a response with the appropriate status code:

```
@POST
@Consumes(MediaType.APPLICATION_JSON)
public Response create(Book book) {
    if (bookshelf.exists(book.getIsbn())) {
        return Response.status(Response.Status.CONFLICT).build();
    }
```

The same goes for `update`; we should check that the updated ISBN matches the ISBN of the book. What we could do here is again set the appropriate status code, which in this case is `BAD_REQUEST`, with a status code of 400:

```
@PUT
@Path("/{isbn}")
public Response update(@PathParam("isbn") String isbn, Book book) {
if (!Objects.equals(isbn, book.getIsbn())) {
        // return
        Response.status(Response.Status.BAD_REQUEST).build();
```

There are other ways of doing this as well. A different approach you could choose is to throw a `WebApplicationException`, which is part of JAX-RS. You give it a reason and you give it a status code which is `BAD_REQUEST` again. For the most common types of `WebApplicationException`, there are predefined subclasses; in this `WebApplicationException`, you can see there are several subclasses available and there's already a `BadRequestException`.

Let's use `BadRequestException` instead, and we're done.
This `BadRequestException` automatically sets the status code to 400 for us:

```
@PUT
@Path("/{isbn}")
public Response update(@PathParam("isbn") String isbn, Book book) {
    if (!Objects.equals(isbn, book.getIsbn())) {
        // throw new WebApplicationException(
        "ISBN must match path parameter.",
        Response.Status.BAD_REQUEST);
        throw new BadRequestException(
        "ISBN must match path parameter.");
    }
}
```

Now that's done, of course there are a lot of other exceptions that can happen, such as custom runtime exceptions and persistence exceptions, that might throw our JPA provider. So, how do we handle those? The most convenient way is to have a `PersistenceExceptionMapper` implementation. Create a class and implement `ExceptionMapper`, and use the exception you want to be handled as a generic type. In this case, it's `PersistenceException`.

The first thing you need to do is annotate it using the `@Provider` annotation. Do that, and then you can implement the custom transformation logic that maps `PersistenceException` to the actual `Response` and the HTTP status code you're expecting. For example, if the exception is an instance of `EntityNotFoundException`, we will return 404, which is `NOT_FOUND`. In case anything else happens, we want to return a custom error response structure. In this case, we use a plain `Map`, a `HashMap`, and maybe set a `code` and a `type`. We include the `message` and as a `Response`, we return to `INTERNAL_SERVER_ERROR`, which is status code 500, and we use `type` as `MediaType.APPLICATION_JSON`:

```
@Provider
public class PersistenceExceptionMapper implements
ExceptionMapper<PersistenceException> {
    @Override
    public Response toResponse(PersistenceException exception) {
        if (exception instanceof EntityNotFoundException) {
            return Response.status(Status.NOT_FOUND).build();
        } else {
```

```
Map<String, String> response = new HashMap<>();
response.put("code", "ERR-4711");
response.put("type", "DATABASE");
response.put("message", exception.getMessage());

return Response.status(Status.INTERNAL_SERVER_ERROR)
        .entity(response)
        .type(MediaType.APPLICATION_JSON).build();
    }
  }
}
```

If we switch to our REST client, we can see those things in action. In case we get an unknown book which should trigger the entity 404 NOT_FOUND exception, this is what we expect. For example, if we issue a wrong update request for a book, we expect HTTP status code **400 Bad Request**, as seen in the following screenshot:

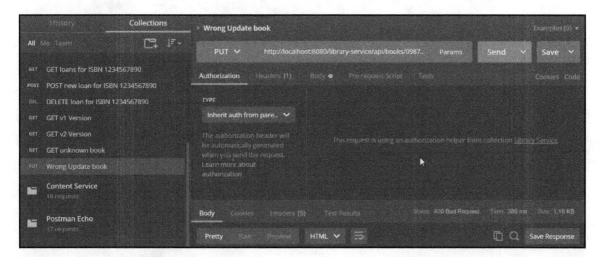

This is it on error handling.

In the next section, we will talk about implementing web service clients with Java EE 8.

Implementing web service clients with Java EE 8

In this section, we're going to take a look at the JAX-RS client APIs and how to implement web service clients. I'm going to show you how you can set up and configure a JAX-RS client instance. We'll use `WebTarget` and its builder to specify request behavior, resolve URI template parameters, do invocation in response handling, and use `GenericType` implementations to get unmarshalled typed collections:

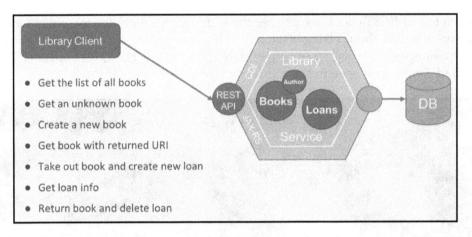

Conceptual view of this section

So far, we've implemented our small library service, which supports books, authors, and loans, via a REST API. We'll then implement a library client which is a standalone client to get a list of books, unknown books, to create books, to get books with the returned URI, and so forth.

Let's switch to our IDE. We will create a small class called `LibraryServiceClient`, which is our standalone application. The first thing we need to do is activate a few dependencies. Most importantly, we want to use the `jersey-client` dependency and we'll also be using the `jersey-media-json-binding` dependency. This is required to implement our standalone application:

```
<dependency>
    <groupId>org.glassfish.jersey.core</groupId>
    <artifactId>jersey-client</artifactId>
    <version>${jersey.version}</version>
    <scope>test</scope>
</dependency>
```

```xml
<dependency>
    <groupId>org.glassfish.jersey.inject</groupId>
    <artifactId>jersey-hk2</artifactId>
    <version>${jersey.version}</version>
    <scope>test</scope>
</dependency>
<dependency>
    <groupId>org.glassfish.jersey.media</groupId>
    <artifactId>jersey-media-json-binding</artifactId>
    <version>${jersey.version}</version>
    <scope>test</scope>
</dependency>
```

The first thing we need to do is construct a JAX-RS client instance, and we use
`ClientBuilder` to do that. Here, when we use `ClientBuilder.newBuilder`, we specify
parameters such as `connectTimeout` and `readTimeout`, we also register
`JsonBindingFeature`, and then finally we call the `build()` method on the builder. Once
we have our `client`, we can use it to construct what is called a `WebTarget`. `WebTarget` is
basically the endpoint we're going to talk to. We use `client.target` and
mention `localhost:8080` because our service is running locally on `localhost:8080`. We
give `path("/library-service/api")`, which is the root of our REST API:

```java
public class LibraryServiceClient {

    private static final Logger LOGGER = Logger.getAnonymousLogger();

    public static void main(String[] args) {
        // construct a JAX-RS client using the builder
        Client client = ClientBuilder.newBuilder()
                .connectTimeout(5, TimeUnit.SECONDS)
                .readTimeout(5, TimeUnit.SECONDS)
                .register(JsonBindingFeature.class)
                .build();

        // construct a web target for the library service
        WebTarget api = client
            .target("http://localhost:8080")
            .path("/library-service/api");
```

To obtain a list of books, we can use this `WebTarget` for the invocation by importing a few things here. What we do is we use `api.path("/books").request`, accept `MediaType.APPLICATION_JSON`, and then we get a list of books. Because this is a generically typed list, we need to use the `GenericType` construct.

We then create a `GenericType` subclass and specify `List<Book>` as the `GenericType` parameter. What if we want to get a book, maybe an unknown book? If we get an unknown book, we expect a status code of 404. Again, we use `api.path("/books").path("/{isbn}");` which is a `path` parameter. Therefore we resolve the template using a specific parameter and value. We use `request`, `accept`, and `get()`. By calling `get()`, we only get the actual `response`, and in that `response`, we use `getStatus()`, which is `404`:

```
LOGGER.log(Level.INFO, "Get list of books.");
List<Book> books = api.path("/books").request()
    .accept(MediaType.APPLICATION_JSON).get(bookList());
books.forEach(book -> LOGGER.log(Level.INFO, "{0}", book));

LOGGER.log(Level.INFO, "Get unknown book by ISBN.");
Response response = api.path("/books")
    .path("/{isbn}").resolveTemplate("isbn", "1234567890")
    .request().accept(MediaType.APPLICATION_JSON).get();
assert response.getStatus() == 404;
private static GenericType<List<Book>> bookList() {
    return new GenericType<List<Book>>() {
    };
}
}
```

If we want to create books, we can do that in a similar way. Again, we create a new book and in here we use `api.path("/books").requestMediaType.APPLICATION_JSON`, which specifies the content type of our payload. We use `post(Entity.json(book))` and expect a status code of 201. If you want to get hold of the just-created book, what we can do is obtain the `URI` of the `response`. We get the location and then we use the client again for the target URI, we `request()`, we accept `MediaType.APPLICATION_JSON`, and we get a POJO of the `Book` class. In such a case, we automatically get the unmarshalled book back:

```
LOGGER.log(Level.INFO, "Creating new {0}.", book);
response = api.path("/books")
    .request(MediaType.APPLICATION_JSON)
    .post(Entity.json(book));
assert response.getStatus() == 201;
```

```
URI bookUri = response.getLocation();
LOGGER.log(Level.INFO, "Get created book with URI {0}.",
  bookUri);
Book createdBook = client.target(bookUri)
  .request().accept(MediaType.APPLICATION_JSON)
  .get(Book.class);
assert book.equals(createdBook);
```

This is the basic workings of the JAX-RS client APIs. Last but not least, you should not forget to close the client (`client.close()`) to free up any resources. If you want, you can do some cleanup. Maybe we want to delete the book we created previously. We need the following code to delete the book:

```
LOGGER.log(Level.INFO, "Delete book with URI {0}.", bookUri);
response = client.target(bookUri).request().delete();
assert response.getStatus() == 200;

client.close();
}
```

This is all there is to it for this section. In the next section, we'll talk about testing Java EE 8 web services.

Testing Java EE 8 web services

In this section, we're going to take a look at different test strategies for Java EE 8 web services. We'll talk about testing simple CDI components with plain unit tests and mocks, testing REST resources using the Jersey Test Framework, and we'll see how to do black box integration testing using the Test Containers framework.

So far, we've implemented our library service by offering a REST API for books, authors, and loans. We also implemented the library client. In this section, we'll talk about testing. You can see the test pyramid in the following diagram. At the bottom, there are unit tests. The middle layer is the service layer tests.

At the top level, you have UI layer tests. Unit testing in Java EE is really simple; you can use your standard test frameworks such as JUnit testing, and you may use Mojito or other mocking frameworks to mock any dependencies:

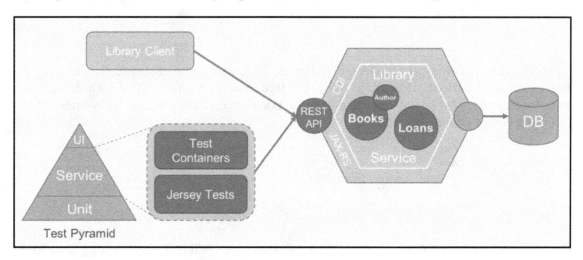

Conceptual view on this section

We won't focus on unit tests here. What's really nice in Java EE is how we can do service level testing. There are two frameworks:

- Jersey Test Framework
- Test Containers framework

Let's use them both.

Jersey Test Framework

Let's start with the **Jersey Test Framework**. We will switch to our IDE and in order to use the Jersey Test Framework, you need to add one simple dependency, as follows:

```
<dependency>
    <groupId>org.glassfish.jersey.test-
      framework.providers</groupId>
    <artifactId>jersey-test-framework-provider-
      grizzly2</artifactId>
    <version>${jersey.version}</version>
    <scope>test</scope>
</dependency>
```

Jersey offers several test providers; in this case, we will be using the `grizzly2` provider. What do you need to do to use this test framework? First of all, you need to implement a test class, say `VersionResourceTest`, and you need to make it extend the `JerseyTest` superclass. Next thing you need to do is override the `configure` method, and what you do here is construct a `ResourceConfig` and pass the resource you want to test. In our case, we want to test `VersionResource`:

```
public class VersionResourceTest extends JerseyTest {

    @Override
    protected Application configure() {
        ResourceConfig config = new
          ResourceConfig(VersionResource.class);
```

The next thing you can do is configure the client that is used to test against our resource. The client here is actually the same one we were using in the previous section, that is, `JsonBindingFeature`, and once you've done that, you can implement the actual tests:

```
    @Override
    protected void configureClient(ClientConfig config) {
        // for JSON-B marshalling
        config.register(JsonBindingFeature.class);
    }
```

If we want to test the `v1` resource, what we can do is specify the target version as `v1`. We use `request` and `target`, and on the `response` returned, we can then specify our usual assertions. Then, assert that the response status code is 200 and that the entity of type string contains the string `"v1.0"`:

```
    @Test
    public void v1() {
        Response response = target("/version/v1").request().get();
        assertThat(response.getStatus(), is(200));
        assertThat(response.readEntity(String.class), is("v1.0"));
    }
```

Now, let's run our test. You can see here that the test is actually firing up a small `grizzly` server that is deploying our resource, and then it's actually firing HTTP calls against our resource. These are the proper integration tests:

```
INFO: Stopped listener bound to [localhost:9998]
Feb 19, 2018 6:55:59 PM org.glassfish.jersey.test.
INFO: Creating GrizzlyTestContainer configured at
Feb 19, 2018 6:55:59 PM org.glassfish.grizzly.http
INFO: Started listener bound to [localhost:9998]
Feb 19, 2018 6:55:59 PM org.glassfish.grizzly.http
INFO: [HttpServer-1] Started.
Feb 19, 2018 6:55:59 PM com.packtpub.javaee8.bound
INFO: Version 2.0 sub resource works.
Feb 19, 2018 6:55:59 PM org.glassfish.grizzly.http
INFO: Stopped listener bound to [localhost:9998]

Process finished with exit code 0
```

Test Containers

Let's look at the next test framework, which is called **Test Containers**. We need to add the following two dependencies to activate the Test Containers framework:

```xml
<dependency>
    <groupId>org.testcontainers</groupId>
    <artifactId>testcontainers</artifactId>
    <version>1.5.1</version>
    <scope>test</scope>
</dependency>
<dependency>
    <groupId>org.slf4j</groupId>
    <artifactId>slf4j-simple</artifactId>
    <version>1.7.25</version>
    <scope>test</scope>
</dependency>
```

The idea behind Test Containers is really simple. Since we're going to deploy our web service in a Docker container anyway, why not use a Docker container during our test as well? All you need to add is a `@ClassRule`. We create `GenericContainer`, we pass it to a `Dockerfile`, we pass it to the WAR file (`library-service.war`) we want to package, we can specify a `Wait` strategy, a `LogConsumer`, and we expose ports. All this code does is fire up a Docker container when this test starts:

```
@ClassRule
public static GenericContainer container =
  new GenericContainer(new ImageFromDockerfile()
      .withFileFromFile("Dockerfile",
        new File(basePath(), "Dockerfile"))
      .withFileFromFile("target/library-service.war",
        new File(basePath(),
        "target/library-service.war")))
      .waitingFor(Wait.forHttp("
        /library-service/api/application.wadl")
            .withStartupTimeout(Duration.ofSeconds(90)))
      .withLogConsumer(new Slf4jLogConsumer(
        LoggerFactory.getLogger(
        LibraryServiceContainerTest.class)))
      .withExposedPorts(8080)
      .withExtraHost("localhost", "127.0.0.1");
```

In the `setUp` phase, what we can do is we can set up a JAX-RS client instance as we've done previously, and once we have the client, we can set up a web target against the container URI. We can ask for the container IP address and the map port of our service, and once we have the web `target`, we can use the JAX-RS client API to interact with our microservice:

```
@Before
public void setUp() {
    client = ClientBuilder.newBuilder()
            .connectTimeout(5, TimeUnit.SECONDS)
            .readTimeout(5, TimeUnit.SECONDS)
            .register(JsonBindingFeature.class)
            .build();

    String uri = String.format("http://%s:%s/library-service/api",
            container.getContainerIpAddress(),
                container.getMappedPort(8080));
    api = client.target(uri);
}
```

Now, run the following command from your console:

```
>mvn integration-test
```

What this does is basically run unit tests and integration tests. First up, the Surefire Plugin tests our version resource, we see everything firing up, it runs the other unit tests, packaging the WAR file. The Failsafe Plugin will run our container integration tests. It'll create and start the container; this might take quite a long time. You can see that the tests completed successfully in the following screenshot:

```
Results:

Tests run: 3, Failures: 0, Errors: 0, Skipped: 0


------------------------------------------------
BUILD SUCCESS
------------------------------------------------
Total time: 02:42 min
Finished at: 2018-02-19T19:00:33+01:00
Final Memory: 15M/491M
------------------------------------------------
```

Summary

Let's summarize what we learned in this chapter. We had a look at basic JAX-RS annotations in order to implement a REST API with CRUD functionality. We used top resource locators to nicely model nested REST APIs. We used HTTP status codes and exception mappers for error handling. We implemented web service clients using the JAX-RS service client API. Finally, we had a look at testing Java EE 8-based web services using several approaches. I hope you enjoyed this chapter. In the next chapter, we will talk about content marshaling with JSON-B and JSON-P.

3
Content Marshalling with JSON-B and JSON-P

In this chapter, we will focus on the data structures and payloads of web services. You will learn how to properly use content types and content negotiation for your web services, how to use the new JSON-B APIs for easy data binding, how JSON-P API can be used for very flexible JSON processing, and how it can be used to implement hypermedia-driven REST APIs.

The following topics will be covered in this chapter:

- Introduction to content types and content negotiation
- Easy data binding using JSON-B
- Flexible JSON processing with JSON-P
- Implementing hypermedia-driven REST APIs

Introduction to content types and content negotiation

In this section, we're going to take a look at using the @Produces and @Consumes annotations to specify the content types. We'll also learn about API versioning using custom content types, smart content negotiation using a quality from server factor, and how you can serve and upload binary content.

Let's switch to code and open our IDE. Let's take a look at the small REST service that we have prepared. As you already know, you can specify the @Produces or @Consumes annotations to specify what your REST service will consume as a content type and what content type your REST service will produce. What we do here is we specify application/json. This is what we usually do. We implement this method and return a simple Map with the status code ok. Using JAX-RS, we'll make sure that this Map is serialized to proper JSON:

```
@GET
@Produces("application/json")
public Response v1() {
    Map<String, String> version =
        Collections.singletonMap("version", "v1");
    return Response.ok(version).build();
}
```

What if we want to implement a second version of this? We can do that by implementing the method called v2 and returning something different:

```
@GET
@Produces("application/json")
public Response v2() {
    Map<String, String> version =
        Collections.singletonMap("version", "v2");
    return Response.ok(version).build();
}
```

Now, this here will not work correctly because we have two methods producing the same content type. What we can do is specify a custom MediaType. We will specify MediaType v1 and MediaType v2 of type "application", and we will use the custom subtype. We have one subtype for version one and the JSON format ("vnd.version.v1+json"), and another one for version two and the JSON format ("vnd.version.v2+json"):

```
public class VersionResource {

    /**
     * MediaType implementation for the version resource in v1.
     */
    public static final MediaType V1 = new MediaType(
      "application", "vnd.version.v1+json");
```

```
/**
 * MediaType implementation for the version resource in v2.
 */
public static final MediaType V2 = new MediaType(
  "application", "vnd.version.v2+json");
```

We can use those custom content types with v1 and v2. Since this is done, we have an API version for v1 and v2 using content types. This is the way it should be if we use an API version. v1 supports application JSON and also supports the content type v1 in the JSON format:

```
@GET
@Produces({"application/json,
  "application/vnd.version.v1+json"})
public Response v1() {
    Map<String, String> version =
       Collections.singletonMap("version", "v1");
    return Response.ok(version).build();
}
```

How does the client specify or know which content type it accepts? Well, basically, they can specify the accept header for this specific content type. If they don't, we specify a factor which is called **quality from server**, that is, qs, qs=0.75, and qs=1. If the client does not specify the content type, "application/vnd.version.v1+json" will always win because it has the higher factor:

```
@GET
@Produces({"application/json; qs=0.75",
  "application/vnd.version.v1+json; qs=1.0"})
```

Let's look at using binary content. We will prepare two methods: serving a JPEG image and a GIF image. All we have to do is just open a file and send the file back:

```
@GET
@Path("/me.jpg")
@Produces("image/jpeg")
public Response jpg() {
    String path = context.getRealPath("/me.jpg");
    return Response.ok(new File(path))
            .header("Content-Disposition", "attachment;
               filename=me.jpg")
            .build();
}
```

```
@GET
@Path("/magic.gif")
@Produces("image/gif")
public Response gif() {
    String path = context.getRealPath("/magic.gif");
    return Response.ok(new File(path)).build();
}
```

What we can also do is implement and upload a mechanism by using the HTTP POST method. We will consume MULTIPART_FORM_DATA. While you are referencing the form with a parameter called "file", which is an input stream, to get the filename, you can also reference @FormDataParam and use FormDataContentDisposition:

```
@POST
@Consumes(MediaType.MULTIPART_FORM_DATA)
public Response upload(
    @FormDataParam("file") InputStream inputStream,
    @FormDataParam("file") FormDataContentDisposition fileInfo) {
        String fileName = fileInfo.getFileName();
        saveFile(inputStream, fileName);

        URI uri = uriInfo.getBaseUriBuilder()
          .path(DocumentsResource.class)
          .path(fileName).build();
        return Response.created(uri).build();
}
```

Now, let's open our REST API. We do not specify anything; we just send the version and receive "v1", which is the default setting:

We also get `"v1"` because I've explicitly set the **Accept** header here:

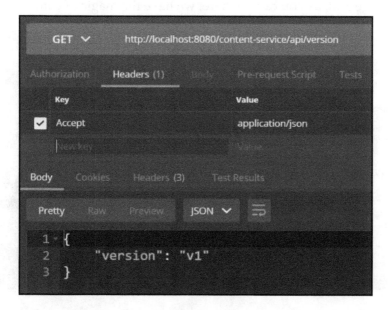

To obtain `"v2"`, we must specify the **Accept** header with the
`application/vnd.version.v2+json` content type:

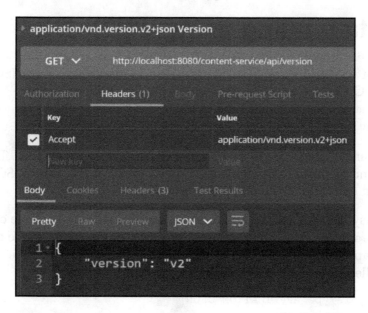

Finally, we can see that the serving of GIF images and JPEGs is also working. We can request a GIF image and, as you can see here, we have the magic of content types:

In the next section, we will talk about easy data binding using JSON-B.

Easy data binding using JSON-B

In this section, we're going to take a look at using JSON-B for marshalling and unmarshalling of your JSON and POJO data structures, how you can use JSON-B annotations on POJOs such as `@JsonbProperty`, `@JsonbNumberFormat`, `@JsonbDateFormat`, `@JsonbTransient`, and `@JsonbPropertyOrder`, and finally how you can explicitly create `JsonbConfig` and `Jsonb` instances using `JsonbBuilder`.

Let's get started and switch to code. We will create a `JsonResource` class. This is our basic REST resource and we want to implement our basic methods that return JSON structures from a POJO and that unmarshall our POJO from JSON structures.

The first bit is easy; first up, we're implementing a basic `@GET` method. We call it `marshall` and it returns a `JsonbPojo`. `JsonbPojo` is a plane POJO object: it's a plane class. We'll use the `@Produces` application for JSON and JAX-RS, and Java EE 8 will make sure that this POJO is marshalled properly to JSON using JSON-B:

```
@Produces(MediaType.APPLICATION_JSON)
public class JsonbResource {
```

```
@GET
public JsonbPojo marshall() {
    return jsonbPojo;
}
```

The same is true for unmarshalling. Let's assume that we want to POST a JsonbPojo to this REST resource. At the class level, we make sure that we use the @Consumes application JSON. If you POST a proper JSON to this REST resource, JAX-RS and Java EE 8 will make sure that this JSON structure is then deserialized and unmarshalled into a JsonbPojo:

```
@POST
public void unmarshall(JsonbPojo pojo) {
    LOGGER.log(Level.INFO, "Default Unmarshalled {0}", pojo);
    this.jsonbPojo = pojo;
}
```

If you don't like the default serialization, what you can always do is take care of the marshalling yourself using the jsonb instance. It offers a method called toJson, which you can pass to any object and it will return the string as an output, and vice versa. You can say that it expects the JSON string as the first parameter and the class of the final POJO as the second parameter. If everything goes the way you want it to, you'll receive the unmarshalled object:

```
@GET
@Path("/custom")
public String marshallCustom() {
    return jsonb.toJson(customJsonbPojo);
}
```

Let's have a closer look at using this jsonb. We will prepare simple unit tests here. What we can always do is create and use JSON-B standalone without any JAX-RS resources. The one thing you should do is use JsonbConfig and make sure that we import everything in there. We will create a new JsonbConfig and on this JsonbConfig, we can set several parameters. For example, you can specify a property ordering strategy where we use LEXICOGRAPHICAL. You can also specify REVERSE and ANY in any case as well. We can specify if we want to marshall null values, use a property naming strategy, in this case, LOWERCASE_CASE_WITH_DASHES, we can specify whether the produced JSON is formatted or not, you can specify a default date format, you can specify how to handle binary data, and you can specify the overall locale. Using jsonbConfig is pretty straightforward; we use the JSON-B builder (JsonbBuilder) and call the create method on it and pass create(jsonbConfig):

```
@Before
public void setUp() throws Exception {
    JsonbConfig jsonbConfig = new JsonbConfig()
```

```
                    .withPropertyOrderStrategy(
                      PropertyOrderStrategy.LEXICOGRAPHICAL)
                    .withNullValues(true)
                    .withPropertyNamingStrategy(PropertyNamingStrategy
                      .LOWER_CASE_WITH_DASHES)
                    .withFormatting(false)
                    .withDateFormat("dd.MM.yyyy", Locale.GERMANY)
                    .withBinaryDataStrategy(BinaryDataStrategy.BASE_64)
                    .withLocale(Locale.GERMANY);

        jsonb = JsonbBuilder.create(jsonbConfig);
    }
```

Once we obtain this JSON-B instance, in the test methods, we use `jsonb.toJson(pojo)` and we get the string JSON-B from JSON. Pass it the string data and a class you want and the `pojo` will be returned:

```
@Test
public void testToJsonWithPlainPojo() {
    PlainPojo pojo = PlainPojo.create();
    String json = jsonb.toJson(pojo);
    assertThat(json).isEqualTo(PLAIN_POJO_JSON);
}
```

This works for plain POJOs and POJOs that have not been specifically annotated. If we want to overwrite these default configurations, we can annotate our POJO like we did previously using `@JsonbPropertyOrder`. For example, to specify the very explicit property order, we can say `@JsonbProperty` to give it a different name, `@JNumberFormat` to specify the number format to use, `@JsonbDateFormat` to specify a different date, or `@JsonbTransient`, which tells JSON-B to ignore this property during marshalling and unmarshalling:

```
@JsonbPropertyOrder(value = {"message",
    "answerToEverything", "today"})
public static class AnnotatedPojo {
    @JsonbProperty(value = "greeting", nillable = true)
    public String message;

    @JsonbNumberFormat("#,##0.00")
    public Integer answerToEverything;

    @JsonbDateFormat("MM/dd/yyyy")
    public LocalDate today;

    @JsonbTransient
    public BigDecimal invisible = BigDecimal.TEN;
```

Let's take this test and run our thing. Our test should hopefully be green, as shown in the following screenshot:

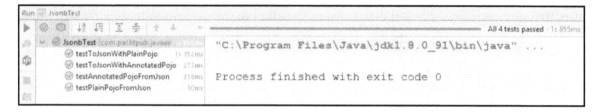

In this section, we saw that using JSON-B is really simple and straightforward. In the next section, we'll talk about flexible JSON processing with JSON-P.

Flexible JSON processing with JSON-P

In this section, we're going to take a look at using JSON-P builders to construct JSON arrays and objects. We'll see how you can use JSON-P in REST resources for marshalling and unmarshalling data, how to use JSON Pointers to access JSON structures, and have a closer look at JSON Patch and JSON Diff to modify JSON structures. We will also be using the @PATCH annotation and the `application/json-patch+json` content type to apply patches in our REST resources, so there's lots of content ahead.

Let's get started. As usual, we prepare a small REST resource as a template to start. The first thing we do is create arrays for JSON and JSON objects using the associated builders, so let's do that:

```
public void testJsonBuilder() {
    JsonArray values = Json.createArrayBuilder()
            .add(Json.createObjectBuilder()
                    .add("aString", "Hello Json-P 1")
                    .add("aInteger", 42)
                    .add("aBoolean", false)
                    .add("aNullValue", JsonValue.NULL)
                    .build())
```

Here, we're using the `createArrayBuilder` to create an array builder, and we're using the `add` method to add JSON objects. Here, you can use `Json.createObjectBuilder` to obtain an object builder. On this object builder, we then call different `add` methods to add a string, an integer, a Boolean, or maybe a null value using the special `JsonValue`. That's all there is to it. Using these two builders, you can create complex JSON structures quite easily.

What do we do with this? The first thing we do is we return `jsonArray`; this is really straightforward. You can explicitly and directly return this `jsonArray` for marshalling. To do this, we will produce an `APPLICATION_JSON` as our content type and JAX-RS will make sure that our `jsonArray` is serialized and marshalled to the corresponding JSON structure:

```
@Produces(MediaType.APPLICATION_JSON)
  @GET
  public JsonArray marshall() {
      return jsonArray;
  }
```

The same is true if we want to unmarshall the data using JSON-P. We will consume the `APPLICATION_JSON`, get the `InputStream` which is basically `jsonBody`, and we're going to use `JsonReader` Here, we're going to use `Json.CreateReader(jsonBody)` from the `InputStream`, obtain a `JsonReader`, and on the `reader`, we can read the array:

```
@POST
@Consumes(MediaType.APPLICATION_JSON)
public void unmarshall(InputStream jsonBody) {
    JsonReader reader = Json.createReader(jsonBody);
    this.jsonArray = reader.readArray();

    LOGGER.log(Level.INFO, "Unmarshalled JSON-P {0}.", jsonArray);
}
```

Let's see what else there is in JSON-P. Well, first up there are JSON Pointers. Let's look into JSON Pointers. Let's assume we have a simple JSON structure. In this test, we'll create a reader using a string, and we'll obtain a `JsonObject` from the reader and a `JsonArray` from this object:

```
@Test
public void testJsonPointer() {
    JsonReader jsonReader = Json.createReader(new StringReader("
      {\"aString\":\"Hello Json-P\",\"arrayOfInt\":[1,2,3]}"));
    JsonObject jsonObject = jsonReader.readObject();
    JsonArray jsonArray = jsonObject.getJsonArray("arrayOfInt");
```

What if we want to access an array value by index? For this, we use a JSON Pointer. We'll use `Json.createPointer`, and using this annotation here basically specifies the path and the index of the value we want to reference. We'll also create a `jsonPointer`, and on the `jsonPointer` we can then set `getValue` and pass it the `JsonObject`.

Doing this, we'll get back a `jsonValue` and what we can do is we can check that the values of the `JsonNumber` and `jsonArray` instances are correct as well:

```
// access an array value by index
JsonPointer jsonPointer = Json.createPointer("/arrayOfInt/1");
JsonValue jsonValue = jsonPointer.getValue(jsonObject);
assertThat(jsonValue).isInstanceOf(JsonNumber.class);
assertThat(jsonValue).isEqualTo(jsonArray.get(1));
```

We can also use the JSON Pointer to replace objects in the array, for example, or in the JSON structure. We use `jsonPointer.replace`, give it the original `jsonObject`, and we specify the new `createValue(42)` value we want to replace the pointer value with:

```
// replace the array value by index
jsonObject = jsonPointer.replace(jsonObject,
    Json.createValue(42));
jsonArray = jsonObject.getJsonArray("arrayOfInt");
assertThat(jsonArray.getInt(1)).isEqualTo(42);
```

We can also use the JSON Pointer to remove things from the JSON's structure. Here, we can use the JSON Pointer, say, on `remove(jsonObject)`, and a new JSON object will be returned. If we check the JSON array, the size is smaller than before:

```
// remove the array value by index
jsonObject = jsonPointer.remove(jsonObject);
jsonArray = jsonObject.getJsonArray("arrayOfInt");
assertThat(jsonArray.size()).isEqualTo(2);
}
```

Something else regarding JSON-P is JSON Patch. We will create a JSON object first, a `jsonReader`, pass it a string, and read the object from the reader. We will create a `JsonPatch`. For this, we will use the `createPatchBuilder` and on the `patch` we want to say, please replace the element `"/aString"` with the `"Patched Json-P."` value and please remove this from `"/arrayOfInt/1"`. Therefore, you can use JSON Patch to specify modifying operations, such as replacing, removing, and adding values to JSON structures. On the `patch`, we call the `apply` method and we'll pass it as a parameter to the JSON structure we want to apply the patch to. This will return a new and modified JSON object. Here, we can make sure that the modification is done properly:

```
@Test
public void testJsonPatch() {
    JsonReader jsonReader = Json.createReader(
      new StringReader("{\"aString\":
        \"Hello Json-P\",\"arrayOfInt\":[1,2,3]}"));
    JsonObject jsonObject = jsonReader.readObject();
```

```
JsonPatch patch = Json.createPatchBuilder()
        .replace("/aString", "Patched Json-P.")
        .remove("/arrayOfInt/1")
        .build();

jsonObject = patch.apply(jsonObject);
assertThat(jsonObject.getString("aString"))
  .isEqualTo("Patched Json-P.");
assertThat(jsonObject.getJsonArray("arrayOfInt")
  .size()).isEqualTo(2);
}
```

Something else that's quite nice is the JSON Diff feature. Let's assume that we have a `source` and a `target` object. As you can see, they're both kind of the same—they have one element called `"aString"`, but the values differ. What we then do is create a `diff`, say, `Json.createDiff(source, target)`, and what we get back is a `JsonPatch` describing the necessary changes it needs to apply to `source` so that we can get the `target` object. If we have a look at our JSON Diff, we can see all that is required is a `replace` operation. For the following path, we do the same with `"/aString"`, and we need to replace the `"value"` with `"xyz"`. If we apply this patch to the `source` object, we get the `target` object, and we do that by taking the `diff` and applying it to the `source`. We get back a new object and we assert that the `source` is equal to the `target`:

```
@Test
public void testJsonDiff() {
    JsonObject source = Json.createObjectBuilder()
      .add("aString", "abc").build();
    JsonObject target = Json.createObjectBuilder()
      .add("aString", "xyz").build();

    JsonPatch diff = Json.createDiff(source, target);
    JsonObject replace = diff.toJsonArray().getJsonObject(0);
    assertThat(replace.getString("op")).isEqualTo("replace");
    assertThat(replace.getString("path")).isEqualTo("/aString");
    assertThat(replace.getString("value")).isEqualTo("xyz");

    source = diff.apply(source);
    assertThat(source).isEqualTo(target);
}
```

You can also use JSON Patch in your JAX-RS resources as well. For this, we have to use the following two annotations. First up, we use @PATCH and then specify @Consumes with a media type of APPLICATION_JSON_PATCH_JSON. The structure we send this in is a JsonArray, and from that JsonArray, we create a jsonPatch that we can use to apply it to our data structures:

```
@PATCH
@Consumes(MediaType.APPLICATION_JSON_PATCH_JSON)
public void patch(JsonArray jsonPatchArray) {
    LOGGER.log(Level.INFO, "Unmarshalled JSON-P Patch {0}.",
      jsonPatchArray);

    JsonPatch jsonPatch = Json.createPatchBuilder(jsonPatchArray)
      .build();
    this.jsonArray = jsonPatch.apply(jsonArray);
    LOGGER.log(Level.INFO, "Patched {0}.", jsonArray);
}
}
```

That was a lot of content for covering JSON-P. In the next section, we are going to implement a hypermedia-driven REST API using what we've learned so far.

Implementing hypermedia-driven REST APIs

In this section, we're going to take a look at how you can traverse REST resources using hypermedia (with links and URIs). We'll see how to use JSON-P to construct hypermedia enabled JSON structures. We'll use the @Context and UriInfo objects to construct resource URIs programmatically. We will also have a look at how to set link headers with URIs on the HTTP response.

Let's get started and switch to our IDE. We will prepare a resource, and this resource will be serving books and authors; both are individual REST resources. Obviously, books are written by authors, so we should be able to navigate from books to the authors and vice versa. This is what we can use hypermedia for.

Navigate to our book resource. In here, we have the method to serve a specific book. First up, we'll obtain the book and then we can construct the URI for this book. createBookResourceUri is the URI to use to reference this book:

```
@GET
@Path("/{isbn}")
public Response book(@PathParam("isbn") String isbn) {
    Book book = books.get(isbn);
```

```
        URI bookUri = createBookResourceUri(isbn, uriInfo);
        URI authorUri = createAuthorResourceUri(book
          .authorId, uriInfo);
        return null;
    }
```

We also want to construct the author URI for this book. If you look in here into one of those methods, you'll see that we use the `uriInfo` object and that we obtain a base URI builder from it. We then use the `path` methods to actually build the final URI. Using these `path` methods, we can construct the path from the `@Path` annotations of our resources and resource methods:

```
static URI createAuthorResourceUri(Integer authorId,
    UriInfo uriInfo) {
    return uriInfo.getBaseUriBuilder()
            .path(HateosResource.class)
            .path(HateosResource.class, "author")
            .path(AuthorResource.class, "author")
            .build(authorId);
}
```

In the final result, we have a URI that references the actual resource:

```
        URI authorUri = createAuthorResourceUri(book
          .authorId, uriInfo);
```

Next up, what we do is create a JSON object from `book` from our `bookUri`, and this is where hypermedia comes into play. Let's have a look at them. We'll use JSON-P to create an object builder and add `"isbn"` and `"title"` to it. However, there's one bit missing and that bit makes the final hypermedia enabled JSON structure. We will add an additional object called `"_links"` which is a JSON object, and this JSON object contains two other JSON objects which are called `"self"` and `"author"`. `"self"` describes the URI of the REST resource itself, which in this case is the type of book. Then, we specify `"author"`, and we give it an `"href"` attribute which points to `authorUri`:

```
        private JsonObject asJsonObject(Book book, URI bookUri,
          URI authorUri) {
          return Json.createObjectBuilder()
                  .add("isbn", book.isbn)
                  .add("title", book.title)
                  .add("_links", Json.createObjectBuilder()
                          .add("self", Json.createObjectBuilder()
                                  .add("href", bookUri.toString()))
                          .add("author", Json.createObjectBuilder()
                                  .add("href",
                                      authorUri.toString()))))
```

```
        .build();
}
```

Finally, we return the JSON object, and on the `response` object you can also set the link HTTP headers as well so that you have two options. You can either specify the link header on the HTTP `response` or embed the URIs, which adds a linked JSON structure here. We've completed the books.

We can pretty much do almost the same thing for authors; the code this is pretty much copy/paste. This kind of follows the same procedure: we get the authors and then construct the URI for the author and the books. We construct our JSON object where we're going to embed the links to `"self"`, which is `"books"` itself, and do the same for the `booksUri`. Finally, you return the response of this JSON object and we can also embed the `link` HTTP headers.

Now, let's put this API to the test. Open our Postman and issue a `GET` request for the list of books. In here, you will see that the book has a title and that it also contains a list of links. For `"self"`, this is the book itself and for `"author"`, we get the author of the book, as shown in the following screenshot:

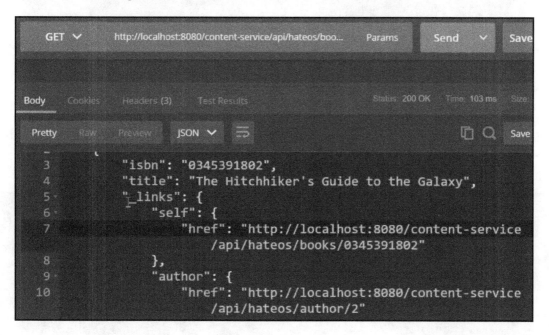

Let's click on the book, that is, the URI present in `"self"`, to get information about this book in particular. As you can see, this returns a single book structure. If you want to navigate to the author, we can use the author link. Here, we have the author of this book, as shown in the following screenshot:

```json
{
    "id": 2,
    "name": "Douglas Adams",
    "_links": {
        "self": {
            "href": "http://localhost:8080/content-service/api
                /hateos/author/2"
        },
        "books": {
            "href": "http://localhost:8080/content-service/api
                /hateos/books?authorId=2"
        }
    }
}
```

If we want to obtain the list of books that this author has written, we can use the `"books"` link, which gets all the books from this author's ID, as shown in the preceding screenshot.

If you want to have a look at this book again, you can navigate from those two books. What you can also see here in the headers is that we have the two links for the author and the book itself:

Summary

Let's summarize what we have learned in this chapter. First up, we had a look at how we can use custom content types and content negotiation in our web services. Next up, we had a look at JSON-B and how we can use it for easy data binding of your POJOs to and from JSON. We also had a look at JSON-P for very flexible JSON processing, and how we can create JSON structures and retrace these structures using JSON-P. Then, we looked at how to use JSON Pointers, JSON Patch, and JSON Diff for more flexible JSON processing, and finally, we had a look at implementing hypermedia enabled REST APIs using JSON-P and `UriInfo`.

In the next chapter, we will talk about building asynchronous web services.

Building Asynchronous Web Services

4

In this chapter, we'll talk about the motivations and reasons for asynchronous processing. Then, we'll see the basic implementation of asynchronous web services with JAX-RS. Then, we will have a look at improving our implementation using `ManagedExecutorService` and server-side callbacks. Finally, we will use the asynchronous JAX-RS API client to make REST calls, and explore the benefits and usage scenarios of asynchronous processing.

This chapter includes the following sections:

- Benefits and usage scenarios of asynchronous processing
- Implementing asynchronous web services
- Using ManagedExecutorService and server-side callbacks
- Implementing asynchronous web service clients

Benefits and usage scenarios of asynchronous processing

In this section, we're going to take a look at the motivations and reasons for asynchronous request processing and why this matters to you. One thing I need to tell you is that *the free lunch is over! concurrency counts*.

Let's take a look at the following diagram:

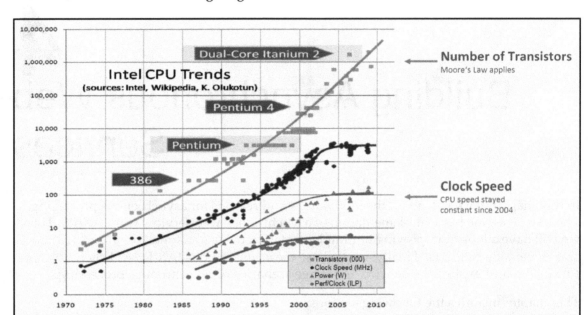

We can see that the number of transistors on a processor is constantly rising; however, the clock speed pretty much stayed constant since 2004. This means you need to be more concurrent in order to get more speed, and we usually do this by using threads.

By default, the request processing on the server usually works in a synchronous mode, which means that each request is processed in a single HTTP thread. This is what we are used to; we had one thread and we performed request responses in it. Unfortunately, threads are very expensive, so under a high load with a lot of concurrent connections, there is a lot of wasted resources and the server does not scale that well. Fortunately, we have asynchronous processing options.

Basic idea

The basic idea of asynchronous processing is to separate our request I/O threads and the request processing threads by using different thread pools. This basically frees up our I/O threads to receive new connections while we do the processing on different threads.

Goal

The ultimate goal is to save memory and improve the performance of our applications by using or reducing context-switching, and we can also improve the throughput by basically separating the request I/O from the request-processing.

These are the main motivations and reasons. In the next section, we will talk about implementing asynchronous web services.

Implementing asynchronous web services

In this section, we're going to take a look at implementing asynchronous REST resources. We'll see the basic usage of the @Suspended annotation and the AsyncResponse class. We'll have a look at processing and resuming on an AsyncResponse instance in a different thread, and we will also talk about the basic timeout-handling for asynchronous responses.

Let's get started and switch to code. As usual, we prepare a few templates for us to get started. First up, I want to show you the basic structure of an asynchronous resource—have a look at the signature. All you need to do is implement a public void method that has at least one parameter that uses the @Suspended annotation. As a type, it uses the AsyncResponse class that's provided by the JAX-RS API:

```
@GET
public void calculate(@Suspended final AsyncResponse
   asyncResponse) {
```

Let's start with the implementation.

We want to do some heavy processing in a separate thread. First up, we'll start a new thread and do the calculation within the thread. To simulate some heavy processing, we'll have it sleep for three seconds, then we'll produce some output. To do that, we return the request thread (requestThreadName). We also need the name of the current thread, and we get that using getCurrentThreadName:

```
asyncResponse.setTimeout(5, TimeUnit.SECONDS);

final String requestThreadName = getCurrentThreadName();

new Thread(() -> {
    try {
        // simulate heavy processing here
        TimeUnit.SECONDS.sleep(3);
    } catch (InterruptedException e) {
```

```
                LOGGER.log(Level.WARNING, "Could not wait for 3s.", e);
            }
            final String responseThreadName = getCurrentThreadName();
```

Finally, we construct a `response` from `requestThread` and `responseThread`:

```
            Map<String, String> response = new HashMap<>();
            response.put("requestThread", requestThreadName);
            response.put("responseThread", responseThreadName);

            asyncResponse.resume(Response.ok(response)
              .build());
        }).start();
    }
```

This is the basic structure of an asynchronous REST resource. We spawn a new thread, process it, construct a `response`, and finally, we call the `resume` method on the `response`.

To be slightly more sophisticated, we can use `BlockingQueue` and we have a method called `lock`, which takes the `@Suspended` asynchronous response. We want to save the asynchronous response to the queue:

```
private LinkedBlockingQueue<AsyncResponse> responses =
  new LinkedBlockingQueue<>();

@GET
public void lock(@Suspended final AsyncResponse asyncResponse)
  throws InterruptedException {
    String currentThreadName = getCurrentThreadName();
    LOGGER.log(Level.INFO, "Locking {0} with thread {1}.",
      new Object[]{asyncResponse, currentThreadName});

    responses.put(asyncResponse);
```

Down here in the `AsyncResource` class, we have an `unlock` method where we want to resume the processing on this currently-locked response. We take `asyncResponse` from the queue—this pulls the asynchronous response from the queue—and then we call the `resume` method on `response`. This will basically resume the previously locked request:

```
@DELETE
public Response unlock() {
    String currentThreadName = getCurrentThreadName();
    AsyncResponse asyncResponse = responses.poll();
```

```
if (asyncResponse != null) {
    LOGGER.log(Level.INFO, "Unlocking {0} with thread {1}.",
      new Object[]{asyncResponse, currentThreadName});
    asyncResponse.resume(Response.ok(Collections.singletonMap(
      "currentThread", currentThreadName)).build());
}

return Response.noContent().build();
}
```

Finally, we want to add some timeout behavior and we can set a specific timeout on `asyncResponse`. If the timeout is exceeded, an HTTP 403 status code is returned:

```
asyncResponse.setTimeout(5, TimeUnit.SECONDS);
asyncResponse.setTimeoutHandler((response) -> {
    responses.remove(response);
    response.resume(Response.status(Response.Status
      .SERVICE_UNAVAILABLE).build());
});
```

If you want to test this, switch to your REST client. First, we send a GET request for the API thread, then we implement it. As we can see here, `"requestThread"` is `http-listener(3)` and `"responseThread"` is a completely different thread:

We do the same thing for the asynchronous GET request; we issue a GET request, which will be blocked. We call the unlock (DELETE) method and get our **204 No Content**, as shown in the following screenshot:

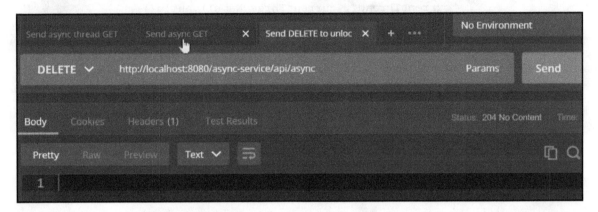

If we switch to the already issued GET request, we get **503 Service Unavailable**, as in this case we waited for too long, as shown in the following screenshot:

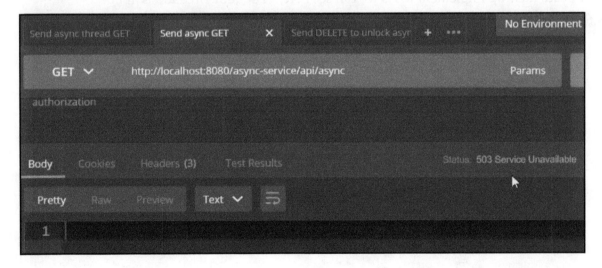

Now, if we call the `DELETE` method and the `GET` method, we see that
the `"currentThread"` is `http-listener(6)`, as shown in the following screenshot:

That's it for this section.

In the next section, we'll see how you can use `ManagedExecutorService` and server-side
callbacks.

Using ManagedExecutorService and server-side callbacks

In this section, we're going to take a look at using a `ManagedExecutorService` instance
for asynchronous request processing. I'm going to show you how to use
`CompletableFuture` to run and resume asynchronous requests. We will talk about using a
`TimeoutHandler` instance for fine-grained timer control, and we'll be using
`CompletionCallback` and `ConnectionCallback` instances for even further control of the
request processing.

Let's get started and switch to code. As usual, we prepare a template project to get started.
The first thing we want to do is use a `ManagedExecutorService` instance. Thus, we will
inject this instance into our REST resource:

```
@Resource
private ManagedEcecutorService executorService;
```

Then, we want to use this `ManagedExecutorService` instance to do some heavy processing, such as processing Fibonacci numbers. We will use the `ManagedExecutorService` instance and call the `execute` method on it. In this `execute` method, we then call `asyncResponse.resume` to resume the asynchronous response and we provide `Response`, which in our case is the requested Fibonacci number:

```
executorService.execute(() -> {
    asyncResponse.resume(Response.ok(fibonacci(i)).build());
    LOGGER.log(Level.INFO, "Calculated Fibonacci for {0}.",
      asyncResponse);
});
```

What else can we do? We should provide and specify the timeout to use, as we saw in Chapter 3, *Content Marshalling with JSON-B and JSON-P*. For this case, we specify a timeout of 10 seconds. We also want to specify a specific timeout behavior, since maybe we do not want to answer with an HTTP status code of 503 in this case. Since we want to specify something different, we can use a `setTimeoutHandler` instance. We will register `setTimeoutHandler` on the asynchronous response, and in case the timeout fires, we resume the response with HTTP status code 202, which is accepted and we just send back a random `UUID`:

```
asyncResponse.setTimeout(10, TimeUnit.SECONDS);
asyncResponse.setTimeoutHandler((r) -> {
    r.resume(Response.accepted(UUID.randomUUID()
      .toString()).build()); //sending HTTP 202 (Accepted)
});
```

We can also register additional callbacks. There are two types of callbacks:

- `CompletionCallback`
- `ConnectionCallback`

We will look at both of them in detail.

CompletionCallback

CompletionCallback is the first callback. It is called by the JAX-RS runtime once the request is completed. The only method you need to implement is onComplete. In case of an error, you will be passed the throwable error and the "Completed processing." parameter, and we can do the required logic in here:

```
static class LoggingCompletionCallback implements
  CompletionCallback {

    @Override
    public void onComplete(Throwable throwable) {
        LOGGER.log(Level.INFO, "Completed processing.", throwable);
    }
}
```

ConnectionCallback

The second type of callback that is optionally supported is ConnectionCallback. Here, you can specify a custom implementation. Currently, the only method you need to implement is the onDisconnect method, which is passed the actual AsyncResponse. This method is called if the client is connected prematurely. According to JSR 339, the support for ConnectionCallback is optional:

```
static class LoggingConnectionCallback implements
  ConnectionCallback {

    @Override
    public void onDisconnect(AsyncResponse disconnected) {
        LOGGER.log(Level.INFO, "Client disconnected on {0}.",
          disconnected);
    }
}
```

Registering callbacks

Once we've implemented the two callbacks, you can register them with the asynchronous response. You can call asyncResponse.register and pass it the class of those callbacks:

```
asyncResponse.register(LoggingCompletionCallback.class);
asyncResponse.register(LoggingConnectionCallback.class);
```

CompletableFuture

Finally, we can use `CompletableFuture` as an alternative syntactic sugar way of using those asynchronous REST APIs. Again, we use a `ManagedExecutorService` instance here. The next thing we want to do is use `CompletableFuture` to run the Fibonacci calculation asynchronously and then apply the `asyncResponse::resume` method. The code will look as follows. Using `CompletableFuture`, we call the `runAsync` method, run our Fibonacci calculation using the supplied `executorService`, and then apply the `asyncResponse::resume` method:

```
@GET
@Path("/{i}")
public void completable(@Suspended final AsyncResponse
  asyncResponse, @PathParam("i") final int i) {
    CompletableFuture
            .runAsync(() -> fibonacci(i), executorService)
            .thenApply(asyncResponse::resume);
}
```

Let's see what this looks like in action. Let's switch to our REST client. First, we call a Fibonacci of 9, which is **34**, as shown in the following screenshot:

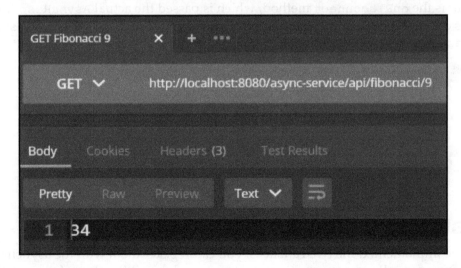

The same goes for Fibonacci at 17, which is 1,597, and so on and so forth. The Fibonacci of 42 takes slightly longer as it is a really long number. We can see what happens if we call the Fibonacci of 49; this is a really big number and it should trigger the timeout of 10 seconds—we expect an HTTP status code of **202 Accepted**, which you can see here, and we get sent back a random UUID response:

In the next section, we will talk about implementing asynchronous web service clients.

Implementing asynchronous web service clients

In this section, we're going to take a look at the basic usage of asynchronous JAX-RS client APIs. We're using `InvocationCallback` instances to react to completed and failed calls. We'll also see how to do invocation-chaining of asynchronous client requests with `CompletableFuture`.

Let's get started and switch to code. As usual, we prepared a small template project to get started. We'll be using a JUnit test to showcase the JAX-RS client APIs. We're going to set up the JAX-RS `client` instance and the JAX-RS `webTarget` instance for the previously implemented asynchronous service API. As you might remember, in the previous section, we used Fibonacci number calculations asynchronously. We'll rewrite the test using the asynchronous JAX-RS client APIs against our REST API.

Let's open the `AsyncWebServiceClientIntegrationTest` class and start our tests; the first test should be pretty easy. We want to construct an asynchronous request and we do this the way we did it before. We use `webTarget.path` and we request `TEXT_PLAIN_TYPE`. Now comes the real difference: we call the `.async()` method and then call `.get(Long.class)`. As you can see, the return type of this call is `Future<long>`. Let's rename it from `longFuture` to `fibonacci` and call the `assertEquals` method on that one:

```
@Test
public void fibonacci17() throws Exception {
    Future<Long> fibonacci = webTarget.path("/fibonacci/17")
      .request(MediaType.TEXT_PLAIN_TYPE).async()
      .get(Long.class);
    assertEquals(1597, (long) fibonacci.get());

}
```

This is pretty much all there is to using asynchronous APIs, though there is slightly more. You can register an invocation callback with `get` to be notified on completed and failed events. Then, we'll see how we implement those callbacks. As you can see, instead of calling `get` for the actual `(Long.class)` type, as we did previously, we call the `get` of `InvocationCallback<Long>`. We can implement the `completed` method for a successful execution and the `failed` method for a failure. Again, we'll return `Future<Long>` for a Fibonacci number and we can then call the `get` method on this `Future`:

```
@Test
public void fibonacci17WithCallback() throws Exception {
    Future<Long> fibonacci = webTarget.path("/fibonacci/17")
      .request(MediaType.TEXT_PLAIN_TYPE).async()
      .get(new InvocationCallback<Long>() {
        @Override
        public void completed(Long aLong) {
            LOGGER.log(Level.INFO,
              "Completed Fibonacci 17 with {0}.", aLong);
        }

        @Override
        public void failed(Throwable throwable) {
            LOGGER.log(Level.WARNING,
              "Completed Fibonacci 17 with error.", throwable);
        }
    });
    assertEquals(1597, (long) fibonacci.get());
}
```

Finally, we'll see how to do invocation-chaining using `CompletableFuture`. This is quite interesting because we can chain several JAX-RS client calls using a `CompletableFuture` fluent API. Imagine we want to calculate the Fibonacci numbers 3, 4, 5, 6, 8, and 21 and do all that in one chain call. This is what it could look like:

```
@Test
public void fibonacci3_4_5_6_8_21() throws Exception {

    CompletableFuture<Long> fibonacci =
            Futures.toCompletable(webTarget.path("/fibonacci/{i}")
                .resolveTemplate("i", 3)
                    .request(MediaType.TEXT_PLAIN_TYPE)
                    .async().get(Long.class))
                .thenApply(i -> webTarget
                    .path("/fibonacci/{i}")
                    .resolveTemplate("i", i + 2)
                        .request(MediaType.TEXT_PLAIN_TYPE)
                        .get(Long.class))
                .thenApply(i -> webTarget
                    .path("/fibonacci/{i}")
    . . .
    . . .
    . . .
    assertEquals(10946, (long) fibonacci.get());
}
```

As you can see, we do the first call and we use the `.async()` method, which returns `Future`. We'll convert this `Future` to a `CompletableFuture`, and then for the next calls, we use `thenApply` and we'll do that for the next one and so on and so forth. This will ultimately make seven calls.

Let's run this test to make sure everything's ready and it'll compile our tests. We can see that the first three are already successful; the `Fibonacci49WithCallback` should result in a 202, and then we're done.

That's all the magic behind the JAX-RS asynchronous line API, as shown in the following screenshot:

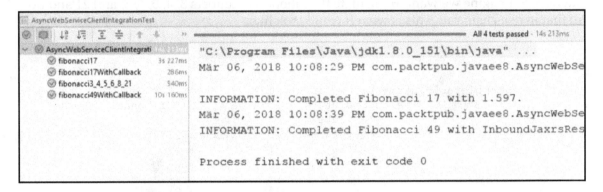

Output showing asynchronous tests running successfully

Summary

In this chapter, we talked about the motivation and benefits of luminous web services, and how they ultimately save memory and improve the performance and throughput of our REST API. We then talked about the basic usage of the @Suspended annotation and the AsyncResponse class. We learned how to use TimeoutHandler and server-side callback instances for fine-grained control. We then used ManagedExecutorService and CompletableFuture for some more syntactic sugar. Finally, we talked about the usage of asynchronous JAX-RS client APIs.

In the next chapter, we'll talk about using server-sent events.

5
Using Server-Sent Events (SSEs)

In this chapter, we're going to take a look at **Server-Sent Events (SSE)**. We will have a look at the characteristics of some usage scenarios, and then we'll be implementing and sending simple SSEs on the server side using JAX-RS. Next up, we'll be implementing SSEs on the client-side using JAX-RS engine HTML and finally, we will have a look at sending and receiving server-sent broadcast events to implement something like a simple HTML chat client.

This chapter includes the following sections:

- What are SSEs?
- Implementing SSE on the server-side
- Implementing SSE REST clients
- Implementing and sending SSE broadcasts

What are SSEs?

In this section, we're going to take a look at SSEs, and take a look at some of its usage scenarios. We'll then be implementing and sending a simple SSE on the server side using JAX-RS. Next up, we'll implement SSE on the client-side using JAX-RS and HTML. Finally, we will have a look at sending and receiving server-sent broadcast events to implement something like a simple HTML chat client.

We're going to take a look at SSEs, what they are, and some usage scenarios. We will also have a look at some differences to other related technologies like WebSockets, Polling, and Long Polling.

So, what are SSEs, exactly? They are a very simple HTTP-based API, dedicated to Push communication, and currently SSEs are implemented in most recent browsers like Firefox, Chrome, Safari, and Opera. Unfortunately, SSEs are currently not implemented in Internet Explorer or Edge.

SSE allows you to send simple text data from the server to the client. One important thing: SSEs are one-way in communication. You might be thinking, *hey, well I've used Polling and Long Polling in the past, and they kind of do the same thing*. The main difference is that with Polling and Long Polling, it is the client that occasionally tries to load new data. With SSE, it's not the client Polling, it's always the server pushing data to the client.

You might have heard of WebSockets before, but WebSockets are a totally different thing. First up, they are TCP-based. They provide a full duplex communication link between the client and the server. Using a WebSocket, the client can always send data to the server and the server can always send data to the client. In SSE, you can think of an event-stream of really simple text data. The text data must be encoded using UTF-8. What we can do in the event-stream is send simple messages and encode these messages. These messages may even be in JSON or you maybe you can only send messages that are plain string or perhaps primitive data. Messages in the event-stream are separated by a pair of newline characters ("\n").

Remember: SSEs are simple Push communication mechanisms, and you can send an event-stream from the server to the client without the client leading to Polling.

In the next section, we're going to have a look at implementing SSE on the server-side using JAX-RS.

Implementing SSE on the server-side

In this section, we're going to take a look at opening SSE sinks using the text/event-stream media type. We'll be sending simple data and also JSON data events. Finally, we'll be closing and disconnecting the SSE sink which we previously opened.

Let's get started, dive into the code, and open our IDE. As usual, we prepare a small template to get us started. Open the `EventsResource.java` file. The first thing we need to do is implement the opening of the event-stream. We can do that by implementing a plain HTTP `@GET` method, though the first thing is going to be the parameter, which is where we pass the `@Context` of type `SseEventSink`.

This is the object that we can use later to send events down to the client. You can also see the @Produces annotation, which is where we use text/event-stream as the MediaType. This is the special media type used to designate SSE:

```
@GET
@Produces(MediaType.SERVER_SENT_EVENTS)
public void openEventStream(
  @Context final SseEventSink eventSink) {
    this.eventSink = eventSink;
}
```

Once we've opened the SSE event-stream, we can implement the sending of events. First up, we start with a simple @POST method. Again, mind the second parameter, which is a @Context object of type Sse. We use this Sse interface later to construct new events. Let's send the first simple event down the event-stream. We do that using the sse context and construct a newEvent using the string message, and we use the send method on the eventSink and send this to the event:

```
@POST
public void sendEvent(String message, @Context Sse sse) {
    final SseEventSink localSink = eventSink;
    if (localSink == null) return;

    // send simple event
    OutboundSseEvent event = sse.newEvent(message);
    localSink.send(event);
```

We can also send named events which can give your events some names. Again, we are using the sse context in order to construct a newEvent. We can see here that we gave it a name (stringEvent) and that we passed in the message as data. Again, we used the localSink and the send method to send this event:

```
// send simple string event
OutboundSseEvent stringEvent = sse.newEvent(
  "stringEvent", message + " From server.");
localSink.send(stringEvent);
```

This also works for other primitive data. Perhaps we want to send the current time in milliseconds. As you can see, there's also a newEventBuilder available in the sse context. We use sse.newEventBuilder, name, and data and call the build method on it. We then call the send method as follows:

```
// send primitive long event using builder
OutboundSseEvent primitiveEvent = sse.newEventBuilder()
        .name("primitiveEvent")
```

```
                  .data(System.currentTimeMillis()).build();
        localSink.send(primitiveEvent);
```

And finally, we can also send JSON events. For example, what we have is a simple POJO implementation using some @JsonbPropertyOrder annotation:

```
@JsonbPropertyOrder({"time", "message"})
public static class JsonbSseEvent {
    String message;
    LocalDateTime today = LocalDateTime.now();
    public JsonbSseEvent(String message) {
        this.message = message;}
    public String getMessage() {
        return message;}
    public void setMessage(String message) {
        this.message = message;}
    public LocalDateTime getToday() {
        return today;}
    public void setToday(LocalDateTime today) {
        this.today = today;}
    }
}
```

Let's send this down the wire. We used the newEventBuilder, we gave it a name, and we passed in an instance of our POJO as data. We can specify the mediaType of this event, which in our case is the application JSON. We can use .build and send it down the event-stream:

```
// send JSON-B marshalling to send event
OutboundSseEvent jsonbEvent = sse.newEventBuilder()
            .name("jsonbEvent")
            .data(new JsonbSseEvent(message))
            .mediaType(MediaType.APPLICATION_JSON_TYPE)
            .build();
    localSink.send(jsonbEvent);
    }
```

That's all there is to sending events. The last thing we need to do is close the event-stream. We can use the HTTP DELETE method for this one. If we call HTTP DELETE on this resource, we can simply call a close method on the eventSink and we're done:

```
@DELETE
public void closeEventStream() throws IOException {
    final SseEventSink localSink = eventSink;
    if (localSink != null) {
        this.eventSink.close();
    }
```

```
    this.eventSink = null;
}
```

Let's put this to the test. Open a browser and navigate to the GET endpoint. As we can see, this call does not return, as it is waiting for events, as shown in the following screenshot:

Now, we open our Postman to send some events and click **Send** a few times. Let's go back to our browser. As we can see, our events have arrived, as shown in the following screenshot:

```
localhost:8080/sse-serv  ×
←  →  ×  ⓘ localhost:8080/sse-service/api/events

data: Hello SSE events!

event: stringEvent
data: Hello SSE events! From server.

event: primitiveEvent
data: 1521533774216

event: jsonbEvent
data: {"message":"Hello SSE events!","today":"2018-03-20T08:16:14.242"}

data: Hello SSE events!

event: stringEvent
data: Hello SSE events! From server.

event: primitiveEvent
data: 1521533776768

event: jsonbEvent
data: {"message":"Hello SSE events!","today":"2018-03-20T08:16:16.769"}
```

That's all there is to implementing services and events on the client-side.

In the next section, we will be talking about implementing service and event REST clients as well as HTTP clients.

Implementing SSE REST clients

In this section, we're going to take a look at registering an JAX-RS client instance to receive SSE. We're going to send messages to the SSE service endpoint, and we want to receive those messages in our JAX-RS client. Finally, we will look at implementing a simple HTML client using JSP.

There's a lot of ground to cover in this section. Let's begin and switch to our IDE. As usual, we will prepare a template project to get us started. What we need to do is implement a small JUnit integration test that we can use as our JAX-RS client. In the `setUp` method, we will first construct an executor (you'll see in a bit why we need one). In order to do this, we will use the JAX-RS `clientBuilder` and construct a `newBuilder`. We wll specify the `connectTimeout` and the `readTimeout` and call the `.build`:

```
@Before
public void setUp() {
    client = ClientBuilder.newBuilder()
            .connectTimeout(5, TimeUnit.SECONDS)
            .readTimeout(30, TimeUnit.SECONDS)
            .build();

    executorService = Executors.newSingleThreadScheduledExecutor();
}
```

What's left is that we need to construct and open the `webTarget` for our REST endpoint. What we do here is use the `client`, we specify the `target` as `localhost:8080` in this case, and we implement the `path` in the `events` endpoint like we did in the *Implementing SSE on the server-side* section:

```
webTarget = client.target("http://localhost:8080")
            .path("/sse-service/api/events");
```

In the `tearDown` method, we close the client and call the `executorService`:

```
@After
public void tearDown() {
    client.close();
    executorService.shutdown();
}
```

Let's implement the receiving of SSE. First, what we need to do is send some solid SSE so that we can try and implement an event loop. We send messages to an endpoint and we receive those messages which are sent. This is what we use the `executorService` for. Therefore in `executorService`, we occasionally send events every 500 milliseconds. We use `executorService.scheduleWithFixedDelay`, and `webTarget.requests`, we call `post`, and we enter some plain text data to our JAX-RS endpoint. As you can see, we have an initial delay of 250 milliseconds, and we do that every 500 milliseconds:

```
@Test
public void receiveSse() throws Exception {

    executorService.scheduleWithFixedDelay(() -> {
        webTarget.request().post(Entity.entity(
          "Hello SSE JAX-RS client.",
          MediaType.TEXT_PLAIN_TYPE));
    }, 250, 500, TimeUnit.MILLISECONDS);
```

Now comes the interesting bit: let's receive those events. First, what we need to do is obtain an `SseEventSource`. We use `SseEventSource.target`, we give it the `webTarget` we previously constructed, and we call `.build`. This gives us an instance of `SseEventSource`. Let's interact with `eventSource`. The first thing we need to do is register a handler that is called whenever we receive an event. To do that, we use `eventSource.register`, and all we do is log the event name and read the data of the event. All that's left is that we need to start receiving those events. To do that, we need to call the `open` method on the `eventSource`. Just to make sure that this test doesn't return immediately, we put in a sleeve of 5 seconds in here:

```
    try (SseEventSource eventSource = SseEventSource
      .target(webTarget).build()) {
        eventSource.register((e) -> LOGGER.log(Level.INFO,
                "Recieved event {0} with data {1}.",
                new Object[]{e.getName(), e.readData()}));
        eventSource.open();

        TimeUnit.SECONDS.sleep(5);
    }
}
```

Let's see if that works. We'll build and run this integration test, which will take some time to compile. We can see that it's receiving the `JsonbEvent`, a simple message, a `primitiveEvent`, and also the `stringEvent` we just expected, as shown in the following screenshot:

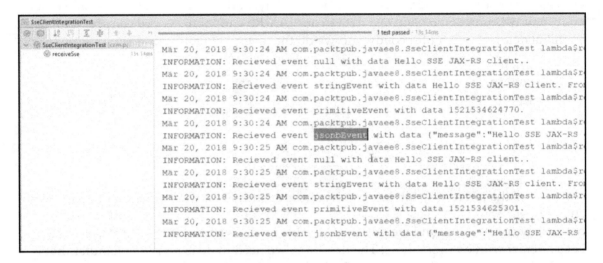

Output of integration tests showing events

This is all there is to sending and receiving SSE using the JAX-RS client. Let's look at one more bit, and that is regarding how you can consume these SSEs using plain HTML and JSP. We will prepare a small JSP showcase and, since most modern browsers support this, it's going to be a good showcase. The first thing you need to do is add some JavaScript, and you need to open the `EventSource`. In JavaScript, you can open the `EventSource` by using `new EventSource`, and we give it the endpoint of our `events` endpoint. To receive normal unnamed events, we have to use the `onmessage`. We register `function` in `source.onmessage` and append the `event.data` to a `div` that we defined at the start of the file:

```
<h2>Messages</h2>
<div id="messages"></div>
<script>
    if (typeof(EventSource) !== "undefined") {
        var source = new EventSource(
          "http://localhost:8080/sse-service/api/events");
        source.onmessage = function (event) {
            document.getElementById("messages").innerHTML +=
                event.data + "<br>";
        };
```

For any named events, we have to do this in a slightly different manner. Here, we have to use a different method called the `addEventListener` method on our `source`. We register `addEventListener` for `"sringEvent"`, `"primitiveEvent"`, and `jsonEvent`. We append the data received from the event to the `div` tags we defined at the top of the JSP file:

```
<script>
    if (typeof(EventSource) !== "undefined") {
        var source = new EventSource(
            "http://localhost:8080/sse-service/api/events");
        source.onmessage = function (event) {
            document.getElementById("messages")
            .innerHTML += event.data + "<br>";
        };
    ...
    ...
        source.addEventListener("jsonbEvent", function (e) {
            document.getElementById("jsonbEvents")
            .innerHTML += e.data + "<br>";
        }, false);
    } else {
        document.getElementById("jsonbEvents").innerHTML =
        "Sorry, your browser does not support server-sent events...";
    }
```

Now, let's open a browser and go to the URL (`localhost:8080/sse-service/events.jsp`). This is what our simple UI should look like:

I know it's not very pretty, but it does the job. In the background, the SSE channel to our server has already been opened. If we open our Postman and start to POST some events and go back to our browser page, we can see that those events will appear, as shown in the following screenshot:

We invoke these by sending them three times, and you can see here that we have three times the different messages.

That's all for this section. In the next section, we will talk about implementing and sending SSE broadcasts.

Implementing and sending SSE broadcasts

In this section, we're going to take a look at creating SSE broadcaster instances. We're going to register SSE event sinks with this SSE broadcaster, and then we're going broadcast events to all registered sinks. Finally, we'll implement a simple HTML chat leveraging SSE.

There's a lot of ground to cover in this section. Let's get started and open our IDE. As usual, to get started, we will prepare a small skeleton project. First up, we will implement the `BroadcastResource` class, which is the server side for sending SSE broadcasts. We have a few things to do. We will inject the SSE `@Context` which we need to construct new events. The next thing we need to do is initialize an SSE broadcaster. For this, we will use the `@Context` we just injected and we'll define an `SseBroadcaster` so that this is the main instance. We will also use a `@PostConstruct` initializer to create a `newBroadcaster` using the `sse` context:

```
@Context
private Sse sse;
private SseBroadcaster sseBroadcaster;

@PostConstruct
public void initialize() {
    sseBroadcaster = sse.newBroadcaster();
}
```

The next thing we need to implement is the registering of SSE event sinks with this broadcaster. We will implement a simple `@GET` method for that, but remember it's annotated with the media type `text/event-stream`. All we need to do is call `sseBroadcaster.register` with the `sseEventSink` instance:

```
@GET
@Produces(MediaType.SERVER_SENT_EVENTS)
public void fetch(@Context SseEventSink sseEventSink) {
    sseBroadcaster.register(sseEventSink);
}
```

The last bit that is missing is that we need to be able to broadcast and send SSE events. What we do here is define a POST method that we can use to consume an HTML form (APPLICATION_FORM_URLENCODED) and the @FormParam called "message". We use this to construct an outbound SSE event (OutboundSseEvent) like we did in the previous section. We do this by using sse.newEvent, giving it a name, and passing it the message, and then we use the broadcast method on the sseBroadcaster instance to broadcast the event and we return noContent:

```
@POST
@Consumes(MediaType.APPLICATION_FORM_URLENCODED)
public Response broadcast(@FormParam("message") String message) {
    OutboundSseEvent broadcastEvent = sse.newEvent(
      "message", message);
    sseBroadcaster.broadcast(broadcastEvent);
    return Response.noContent().build();
}
```

That's all for the server side. Let's have a quick look on the HTML side. Again, we will use a really simple plain JSP file for that like we did in a previous section. We will construct an EventSource and we will register an event listener (addEventListener) for our messages. That's all, with only one minor bit missing—we need a simple form to post messages to our BroadcastResource:

```
<form action="/sse-service/api/broadcast" method="post">
    Message <input type="text" name="message"/>
    <input type="submit" value="Submit"/>
</form>
```

Let's put this to the test. We will open up a couple of browser instances to see our super fancy HTML chat client:

Let's enter `Hello Window 1` and click on **Submit**, as follows:

What we expect is to see this message in the second window. You should see the same message in the second window. From the second window, we will type a message `Hello from Window 2` and click **Submit**. Now, if we switch tabs to the first window, we should be able to see the **Hello from Window 2** message sent from the second window, as follows:

You might think that this is faked, but it isn't. Let's open Postman and use it to also send messages to this broadcast resource. If you look at **Headers**, we have the Content-Type already mentioned, and we have a message under the **Body** tab. We will use Postman to send those events, and what we expect is to see this message in the browser windows. Let's click once, maybe twice, maybe three times. Let's switch back to our browser and you will see **Hello SSE broadcast from Postman**, as shown in the following screenshot:

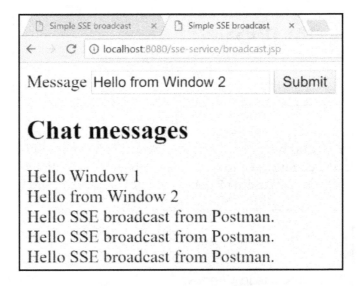

This proves that we have verified that this is a real broadcast working over several client types.

Summary

That's it for this chapter. So, what did we have a look at? First up, we had to look at usage scenarios of service and events and we talked about what SSEs are and other related technologies. Next up, we implemented the sending of services events on the server side with JAX-RS. Then, we had a look at implementing SSE clients and receiving those events using JAX-RS client APIs as well as HTML. Finally, we implemented the sending of SSE broadcasts on the server side and we implemented a small HTML chat client.

In the next and final chapter, we will have a look at advanced REST APIs.

6
Advanced REST APIs

In this chapter, we're going to take a look at adding designs to a REST API using contract and validation. Then, we will learn about using JSON Web Tokens for authentication. And finally, we'll explore diagnosability, that is, logging, metrics, and tracing for a REST API. In this chapter, we'll cover the following topics:

- Applying Design by Contract—adding validation
- Using JSON Web Tokens for authentication
- Diagnosability—logging, metrics, and tracing

Applying Design by Contract – adding validation

In this section, we're going to take a look at adding validation to the `@PathParam` annotation using Javax validation annotations. We will be adding validation POJOs and `POST` bodies using Javax validation annotations. I'm going to show you how to send the HTTP 404 status code for bad and invalid requests.

Let's switch to our IDE. As usual, we will prepare a small template project to get started. We create a `BookResource` similar to the one created in the previous Chapter 5, *Using Server-Sent Events (SSEs)*. There's one thing missing though: there's nothing that tells the API that the ISBN is valid. Let's assume we wanted to add a validation for the ISBN and make sure that it's always 10-characters long and that it only contains digits. Of course, we could program this manually, but there's a better approach.

Instead, we can use Javax validation for this. Let's do that by adding the @Pattern annotation. If you hover over the @Pattern annotation in your IDE, you'll see that this annotation comes from the Javax validation constraints package. We want to use @Pattern to say that we want a regular expression (regexp) only [0-9], and it needs to be 10-digits long; that's all you need to validate the ISBN in this case:

```
@GET
@Path("/{isbn}")
public Response book(@PathParam("isbn") @Pattern(
  regexp = "[0-9]{10}") String isbn) {
    Book book = Optional.ofNullable(books.get(isbn))
                  .orElseThrow(NotFoundException::new);
    return Response.ok(book).build();
}
```

We have the @POST method to create a new book, and we are unsure whether the book sent is valid. First, we add a Javax validation (@Valid) annotation. In this case, we use @Valid, which refers the validation to the annotations within the Book class:

```
@POST
@Consumes(MediaType.APPLICATION_JSON)
public Response create(@Valid Book book,
  @Context UriInfo uriInfo) {
    books.put(book.isbn, book);

    URI uri = uriInfo.getBaseUriBuilder()
      .path(BooksResource.class).path(book.isbn).build();
    return Response.created(uri).build();
}
```

The Book class has an isbn and a title but no Javax validation annotations. The ISBN should be a valid ISBN and the title should neither be null nor blank. We add the @NotBlank and @NotNull annotations for the title and @Pattern of isbn:

```
public static class Book {

        @Pattern(regexp = "[0-9]{10}")
        private String isbn;
        @NotNull
        @NotBlank
        private String title;
```

Let's put this to the test. Let's open our Postman client and try out the **GET Books list** API. We see here that we get one book back:

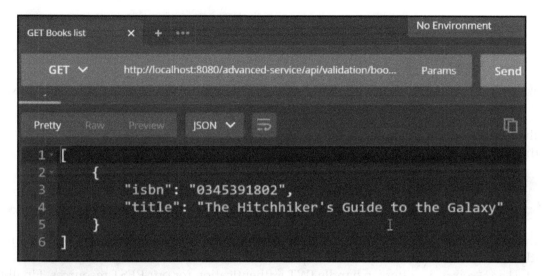

Now let's try to get a book with an invalid ISBN and see what happens; click on the **GET Invalid Book** API (`http://localhost:8080/advanced/books/4711`). You see `4711` in the URI we pass, which is not a valid ISBN because it's not 10-digits long. If we send this, we expect that the server will send us back a bad request; this tells us the request we sent is not valid. If we request a valid book (**GET Valid Book**), we get status **200 OK**, which means the first validations work.

Let's create a new valid book by requesting **POST new valid book**; we can see it has a valid ISBN—10-digits long—and a title. We send this and we get status code **201 Created** back, as shown in the following screenshot:

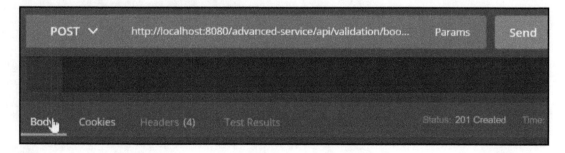

Now let's create an invalid book by requesting **POST invalid book**. Have a look at the **Body**; you'll see an empty `title` and an invalid `isbn`:

```
{
    "isbn": "1234560".
    "title": ""
}
```

If we send this request, we get **400 Bad Request**; the server will not accept any bad books that do not comply with our validation annotations.

In the next section, we're going to have a look at using JSON Web Tokens for authentication.

Using JSON Web Tokens for authentication

In this section, we're going to take a look at decoding **JSON Web Tokens** (**JWTs**) using the Auth0 library. We'll see how you can implement and use the `ContainerRequest` and `ContainerResponse` filters to handle JWT authentication for our REST resources. Finally, we'll be injecting and using decoded JWT in our REST resources.

Let's get started. If you visit the JWT website (`https://jwt.io/`), you can find relevant information about JWT. Under **Debugger**, you can see what a JWT looks like. We can see the token under **Encoded**—it consists of a **HEADER**, **PAYLOAD**, and **VERIFY SIGNATURE**. This JWT uses symmetric encryption to generate the signature. Therefore this value will later be transmitted by the HTTP authorization header:

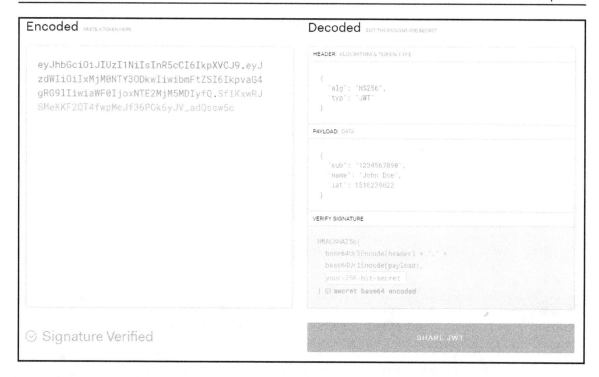

As usual, we prepare a small template project to get started. First, we activate a third-party library, which is required to handle JWT and decode it. We do that by adding the following dependency in the POM file:

```
<dependency>
    <groupId>com.auth0</groupId>
    <artifactId>java-jwt</artifactId>
    <version>3.3.0</version>
</dependency>
```

Next, we need to implement the `ContainerResponse` and `ContainerRequest` filters; we do that in the `JwtAuthzVerifier` class. We let the `JwtAuthzVerifier` class implement `ContainerRequestFilter` and `ContainerResponseFilter`:

```
@Provider
public class JwtAuthzVerifier implements ContainerRequestFilter,
ContainerResponseFilter {
```

Let's implement those two methods. We need to implement `filter`. To do so, we extract the authorization header from `requestContext` and then decode the bearer token (`decodeBearerToken`):

```
@Override
public void filter(ContainerRequestContext requestContext) {
    try {
        String header = getAuthorizationHeader(requestContext);
        decodeBearerToken(header);
    }
```

To obtain the request header, we use `ContainerRequestContext` and extract `AUTHORIZATION_HEADER`:

```
private String getAuthorizationHeader(
  ContainerRequestContext requestContext) {
    return requestContext.getHeaderString(AUTHORIZATION_HEADER);
}
```

Once we have that, we can decode the bearer token. This is where we will use the Auth0 library. We've provided a bit of verification code, which is basically programming against the used library. Finally, on the response, we will throw away the decoded JWT:

```
private void decodeBearerToken(String authorization) {
    String token = extractJwtToken(authorization);
    Verification verification =
      JWT.require(getSecret()).acceptLeeway(1L);
    DecodedJWT jwt = verify(token, verification);
    decodedJWT.set(jwt);
}
```

That's almost it, but a couple of things are missing. We need to annotate `@Provider` under `@ApplicationScoped`. We also need an annotation that will be active, so we call `@JwtAuthz`:

```
@ApplicationScoped
@JwtAuthz
@Provider
```

Let's have a look at the @JwtAuthz annotation. So far, this is a very basic annotation, but we need a special annotation. We need the @NameBinding annotation. Basically, this annotation binds the annotated @Provider, which we've done in the JwtAuthzVerifier class. In this case, we can put the @Target annotation on a TYPE, which is the REST resource, or a REST method:

```
@NameBinding
@Retention(RetentionPolicy.RUNTIME)
@Target({ElementType.TYPE, ElementType.METHOD})
public @interface JwtAuthz {
}
```

Next, we need to activate our resource and the verifier. Let's jump to AuthenticationResource and to the last final bit. We need to activate our JWT filter for this resource. We do that using the @JwtAuthz annotation directly on the resource:

```
@Path("/jwt")
@JwtAuthz
public class AuthenticationResource {
```

Then we inject the decoded JWT:

```
@Inject
private DecodedJWT decodedJWT;
```

Finally, we add an authenticate method. We obtain the claims (decodedJWT.getClaims()) of the decoded JWT. We construct a response and echo the name and subject claims:

```
@GET
@Path("/authenticate")
public Response authenticate() {
    Map<String, Claim> claims = decodedJWT.getClaims();

    JsonObject response = Json.createObjectBuilder()
            .add("name", claims.get("name").asString())
            .add("subject", claims.get("sub").asString())
            .build();

    return Response.ok(response).build();
    }
}
```

Let's switch to our REST client. If you want to access this resource, go to the path of our `authenticate` resource. Here, we've prepared an `Authorization` header, and in the **Value** we use `Bearer` as a token type followed by the JSON Web Token in encoded format. When we send this, we should expect the **200 OK** status. You should see the decoded `name` and `subject` claims:

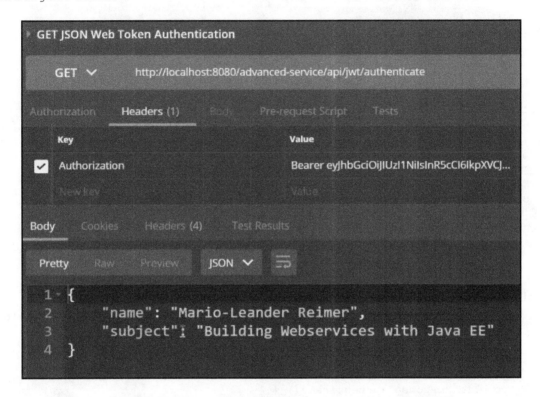

Let's assume we changed the **Value** of the `Authorization` header to `Bearer notvalid`. If we send this, we should get **401 Unauthorized** and the `Invalid JWT token.` message. We just secured our REST API using a simple JWT authentication:

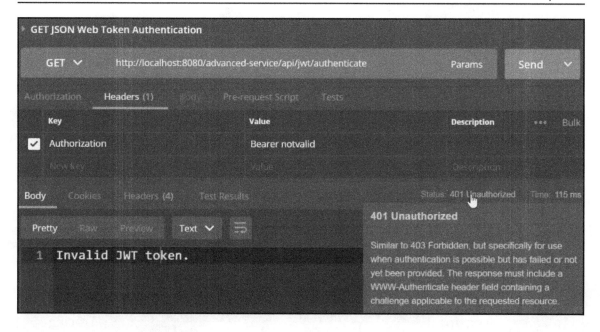

In the next section, we will talk about diagnosability and adding logging, metrics, and tracing to your REST APIs.

Diagnosability – logging, metrics, and tracing

In this section, we're going to take a look at adding request-and-response logging using the Jersey logging feature. We'll have a look at using MicroProfile 1.2 APIs to add metrics and health endpoints. Finally, we'll see how we can include tracing with the OpenTracing API and Jaeger.

Before we start, let's have a quick look at the diagnosability triangle. Diagnosability is really important when it comes to developing web services and distributed applications. When people talk about metrics, you might have heard of Prometheus; when it comes to logging, maybe you've heard about Fluentd; and for tracing, OpenTracing is the most state-of-the-art API out there. Make sure you have a look at these technologies and their stacks.

Let's explore the diagnosability triangle for a small web service:

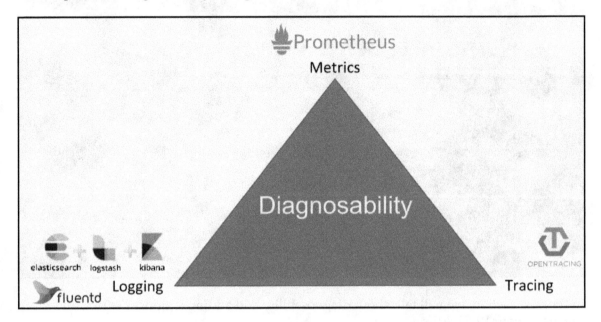

The diagnosability triangle

Let's open the IDE to get started. Open the POM file and add a few dependencies. The first dependency we want to enable is the `jersey.core` or `jersey-common` dependency. This is where the logging feature and the logging filter reside:

```
<dependency>
    <groupId>org.glassfish.jersey.core</groupId>
    <artifactId>jersey-common</artifactId>
    <version>2.26</version>
    <scope>provided</scope>
</dependency>
```

To enable request-and-response logging for every request, we activate `LoggingFeature` in the `JAXRSConfiguration` class:

```
        classes.add(MetricsResource.class);
        classes.add(LoggingFeature.class);

        return classes;
    }
```

If you hover over `LoggingFeature` in our IDE, you can see that it comes from the `jersey-common` module; usually this is already provided so we don't need to write it—no extra dependency to add. The final thing we want to do is modify `LoggingFeature`. Here, we add a few extra properties and we're done:

```
properties.put(LoggingFeature.LOGGING_FEATURE_LOGGER_NAME,
    "RequestLogger");
properties.put(LoggingFeature.LOGGING_FEATURE_LOGGER_LEVEL,
    Level.INFO.getName());
```

This will log every request and every response to your log file. Be careful; it will produce some seriously large logs. Next, we look at how we can use MicroProfile APIs to add metrics and health checks.

Let's switch to our POM and activate MicroProfile APIs. Since we're using Payara micro edition, those APIs are also available to us. There are APIs for health checks, metrics, fault-tolerance if you need it, and for JWT Auth if you don't want to implement this yourself. We need to add the following dependencies in our POM file (the entire code can be found at `https://github.com/PacktPublishing/Building-RESTful-Web-Services-with-Java-EE-8`):

```
<dependency>
    <groupId>org.eclipse.microprofile.health</groupId>
    <artifactId>microprofile-health-api</artifactId>
    <version>1.0</version>
    <scope>provided</scope>
</dependency>
...
...
<dependency>
    <groupId>org.eclipse.microprofile.jwt</groupId>
    <artifactId>microprofile-jwt-auth-api</artifactId>
    <version>1.0</version>
    <scope>provided</scope>
</dependency>
```

Let's go to `MetricsResource` and add a few metrics. This is actually really straightforward. Imagine you have a REST resource and you're interested in how long it took for the invocation of the `POST` request. For this, you can add the `@Timed` annotation. We specify we want the `unit` in `"milliseconds"` and MicroProfile will make sure that every invocation is timed:

```
@POST
@Path("/timed")
@Timed(displayName = "Timed invocation", unit = "milliseconds")
```

It's even easier if you just want to count invocations. For this, we can use the `@Counted` annotation:

```
@POST
@Path("/counted")
@Counted(monotonic = true)
```

Finally, if you're interested in the current absolute value, you can use `@Gauge`:

```
@Gauge(displayName = "Gauge invocation", unit = "seconds")
public long gauge() {
    return poolSize.get();
```

So `@Counted`, `@Gauge`, and `@Timed` are the three metric annotations you can use.

Maybe we also want to add some health checks, because a good microservice should provide health checks. We can specify an `@ApplicationScoped` bean. We annotate it using `@Health`, which implements `HealthCheck`; this comes from the MicroProfile API. Then we implement our basic health-check logic:

```
public class EverythingOkHealthCheck implements HealthCheck {
    @Override
    public HealthCheckResponse call() {
        return HealthCheckResponse
                .named("everythingOk")
                .up()
                .withData("message", "Everything is OK!")
                .build();
    }
}
```

The last thing is tracing—this is a really complicated issue. I want to show you how we can add tracing to your web service. First, we add the tracing API, then we add Jaeger as the tracing implementation. We also use a special annotation to add OpenTracing to JAX-RS 2:

```
<dependency>
    <groupId>io.opentracing</groupId>
    <artifactId>opentracing-api</artifactId>
    <version>0.31.0</version>
</dependency>
<dependency>
    <groupId>com.uber.jaeger</groupId>
    <artifactId>jaeger-core</artifactId>
    <version>0.25.0</version>
</dependency>
<dependency>
    <groupId>io.opentracing.contrib</groupId>
```

```
        <artifactId>opentracing-jaxrs2</artifactId>
        <version>0.1.3</version>
    </dependency>
```

These are the required dependencies. After this we just need to activate the tracer. This is done in only a couple of lines of code. We construct a tracing `Configuration` from the environment. We register this `Configuration` and `getTracer` using `GlobalTracer`:

```
@WebListener
public class OpenTracingContextInitializer implements
ServletContextListener {
    @Override
    public void contextInitialized(ServletContextEvent sce) {
        Configuration configuration = Configuration.fromEnv();
        GlobalTracer.register(configuration.getTracer());
    }
}
```

Let's see what our web service looks like.

Open Postman and issue a few requests, such as **POST Timed Metric** and **POST Counted Metric**. **POST Timed Metric** invokes the `@Timed` request. **POST Counted Metric** invokes the `@Counted` request; we invoke this one a couple of times.

We invoke the **GET Metrics** endpoint, which is provided automatically by the MicroProfile implementation. We issue our metrics and we can see our custom metrics, such as `MetricsResource.gauge`, `MetricsResource.timed`, and `MetricsResource.timed`.

If we don't want JSON and want to use Prometheus, we can do that by invoking the **Metrics for Prometheus** GET request. We can see the Prometheus metrics data automatically provided.

You can also invoke the **GET Healthcheck** request to see whether everything is okay, we should get the following Body in Postman:

```
{
    "outcome": "UP"/
    "checks": [
        {
            "name": "everythingOk",
            "state": "UP",
            "data": {
                "message": "Everything is OK"
            }
        }
    ]
}
```

Everything is working and we're done.

Summary

In this chapter, we looked at validating REST API parameters and payloads using Javax validation. We learned how to add JWT paste authentication to a REST service and decoded JSON Web Tokens manually. Finally, we talked about adding, logging, and metrics, and tracing using Jersey, MicroProfile, and other open source components.

Other Books You May Enjoy

If you enjoyed this book, you may be interested in these other books by Packt:

Architecting Modern Java EE Applications
Sebastian Daschner

ISBN: 978-1-78839-385-0

- What enterprise software engineers should focus on
- Implement applications, packages, and components in a modern way
- Design and structure application architectures
- Discover how to realize technical and cross-cutting aspects
- Get to grips with containers and container orchestration technology
- Realize zero-dependency, 12-factor, and Cloud-native applications
- Implement automated, fast, reliable, and maintainable software tests
- Discover distributed system architectures and their requirements

Java EE 8 and Angular
Prashant Padmanabhan

ISBN: 978-1-78829-120-0

- Write CDI-based code in Java EE 8 applications
- Build an understanding of Microservices and what they mean in Java EE context
- Use Docker to build and run a microservice application
- Use configuration options to work effectively with JSON documents
- Understand asynchronous task handling and writing REST API clients
- Explore the fundamentals of TypeScript, which sets the foundation for working on Angular projects
- Use Angular CLI to add and manage new features
- Use JSON Web tokens to secure Angular applications against malicious attacks

Leave a review - let other readers know what you think

Please share your thoughts on this book with others by leaving a review on the site that you bought it from. If you purchased the book from Amazon, please leave us an honest review on this book's Amazon page. This is vital so that other potential readers can see and use your unbiased opinion to make purchasing decisions, we can understand what our customers think about our products, and our authors can see your feedback on the title that they have worked with Packt to create. It will only take a few minutes of your time, but is valuable to other potential customers, our authors, and Packt. Thank you!

Index

flexible JSON, processing 49, 50, 51, 52, 53

L

logging
  implementing, with Jersey 95, 96, 97, 98, 99

M

ManagedExecutorService
  using 65, 66
metrics
  adding, with MicroProfile API 95, 97, 98, 99
MicroProfile API
  metrics, adding 95, 96, 97, 98, 99

O

OpenTracing API
  used, for implementation of tracing 95, 97, 98,
    99

Q

quality from server 43

R

REST APIs
  implementing, with JAX-RS 20, 22, 24

S

Server-Sent Events (SSE)
  about 73, 74

implementing, on server-side 74, 75, 76, 78
server-side callbacks
  CompletableFuture 68, 69
  CompletionCallback 67
  ConnectionCallback 67
  registering 67
  using 65, 66
SSE broadcasts
  implementing 83, 84, 85, 86
  sending 83, 84, 85, 86
SSE REST clients
  implementing 78, 79, 80, 82
sub-resources
  using 24, 26, 27, 28

T

Test Containers
  Java EE 8 web services, testing 38, 39
tracing
  implementing, with OpenTracing API and Jaeger
    95, 97, 98, 99

V

validation
  adding, with Javax validation annotations 87, 88,
    89, 90

W

web service clients
  implementing, in Java EE 8 32, 34, 35

www.ingramcontent.com/pod-product-compliance
Lightning Source LLC
Chambersburg PA
CBHW080539060326
40690CB00022B/5176